SECRETS OF THE
PASSING-DRIBBLING GAME
OFFENSE

SECRETS OF THE
PASSING-DRIBBLING GAME
OFFENSE

Burrall Paye

PARKER PUBLISHING PUBLISHING COMPANY, INC.
West Nyack, N.Y.

© 1976 *by*

Parker Publishing Company, Inc.

West Nyack, N.Y.

Library of Congress Cataloging in Publication Data

Paye, Burrall,
    Secrets of the passing-dribbling game offense.

    Includes index.
    1. Basketball--Offense. I. Title.
GV889.P39   796.32'32   75-45060
ISBN 0-13-798041-8

Printed in the United States of America

To Mom

Also by the Author

The Winning Power of Pressure Defense in Basketball

How These Secrets Will Benefit You

Basketball coaches have long needed an offensive system that will work against every conceivable defense. They have been on the periphery of one for years. This book is an attempt to codify rules for such an offensive system. These guides will give the players freedom of movement, yet allow the coach complete control over what is happening on the attacking end of the court.

During the planning months prior to the season, every offensive minded coach in the world faces the same question: what shall I do offensively this season? The coach usually evaluates his returning personnel and builds his system around that evaluation. Many times this means changing an offense completely or trying to remake the returnees into something they are not so that they will fit into last year's structure.

A coach cannot effectively change a player into something he is not. To try is foolish. So why not accept a player as he is, and add only a few additional skills that complement his physique and development. The passing-dribbling game incorporates this concept completely, for the players do what is natural for them, what they have done for years on the playgrounds. Of course, the coach may have to alter a few fundamental skills that the youngster has been doing wrong. But the coach should be selective here. If the boy is performing those skills well, though unorthodoxly, do not change him. The player should be changed only if it insures substantial improvement over the long run.

It is equally foolish to change patterns year after year. Not only is it impossible for the players to fully blend their skills into an effective offense in one year, but it takes the coach several years to understand any offense well enough to teach it to maximum benefit.

One of the three basic beauties of the passing-dribbling game is its adaptability to any current squad roster without massive pattern changes. No other offensive system surpasses the year-to-year carry-over value of the passing-dribbling game. In fact, a coach can adopt the passing-dribbling game into his current system without making serious adjustments.

7

Another advantage is that the passing-dribbling game can be run against all known full court and half court basketball defenses with only minor adjustments. It can be run as a stall, a freeze, or from out of bounds. Think of the practice time that can be saved using this offense.

The third basic beauty is its versatility and simplicity. It can be run as a rule offense *(see Chapter 6)*, as a patterned offense *(see Chapters 7, 8, and 9)*, or as a free style offense (see the entire book). The passing-dribbling game has only three patterns, but those patterns are run skillfully from eight formations *(see Chapter 1)*. This gives us twenty-four plays. And if we wish to invert the offense, that gives us twenty-four more. The patterns can be learned easily and efficiently in a two-hour practice session.

All the offensive drills that we used to produce our State Championship have been presented in simplified form and in a logical order so that they can be taught easily to other squads. Separate sections throughout the book will show how the passing-dribbling game will defeat any defense used against it. The book includes all the little techniques and secrets that the coach must know to teach competently the passing-dribbling game.

The offense is presented in its entirety, developed step-by-step, in all three forms: rule, patterned, and free-style. The coach can instruct his athletes by any or all three methods. He can add this system to his as an auxiliary offense, or he can use the passing-dribbling game as his entire offense. Or the passing-dribbling game can be taught as drills to all players just to develop that illusive championship quality known as savvy.

The style of basketball explained in the following pages is pure rather than transitory. It can be observed being played on the playgrounds of the world. It will not come and go as the fads do. It will be here long after the last pattern has been run. It is *Basketball*.

Burrall Paye

Contents

5   Developing the Two and Three Men Options of the Passing-Dribbling Game • 107

Secrets to Breaking Down the Passing-Dribbling Game Offense

Eight Methods of Beginning the Offense

The Two Men Game

The Cuts

The Give and Go
The Backdoor
The Middle Cut
The Go Behind
The Flash Pivot
The Buttonhooks

The Screens and Picks

Screen and Roll
The Blind Pick
The Inside Screen
The Dribbling Screen
The Screen and Go Behind
Secrets of the Explosive Blast
The Screen Down with a Roll

The Three Men Game

Action Involving the Ball
Action Away from the Ball

The Offside Screen
The Pass and Screen Away
The Vertical Rub-Off
The Lateral Rub-Off
The Multiple Screen

Summary

6   The Passing-Dribbling Game: Secrets of Its Rules and Automatics • 126

Initial Group Strategy for the Passing-Dribbling Game

Fundamental Rules

No Two People Cut to Same Spot at Same Time
Anytime a Player's Motion Stops, He Will Be Benched
The Dribble Must Be Kept Alive Between Any Ball Handler and Two Attackers
When Dribbling Toward a Teammate, That Teammate Must Clear the Area or Break Toward the Dribbler

Basic Rules

Strongside Guard Cuts First

SECRETS OF THE
PASSING-DRIBBLING GAME
OFFENSE

CHAPTER 1

What Is the
Passing-Dribbling Game?

The myriad of basketball defenses, growing in number with each new season, has complicated offensive preparations. Some coaches answer this demand by devising an offensive play for each defense to be faced; others have given up and are free-styling completely. Those coaches who free-style have no control over their offensive system. Those who devise many patterns often confuse and limit the effectiveness of their players.

The passing-dribbling game permits players to free-lance; yet it will allow the coach to keep total control over his attack. There are no complicated patterns to learn, only a few simple rules. The next two hundred or so pages will not only acquaint the reader with those precepts, but those pages will show the coach step by step, thoroughly and completely, how to teach and how to apply them.

ADVANTAGES OF THE PASSING-DRIBBLING GAME

Changing offenses year after year does not make sense. Neither the coach nor his players can master an offense in that span of time. When the coach installs the passing-dribbling game, he will have no further need to make drastic adjustments each new season. Its year-to-year carry-over value is unsurpassed by any other offensive attack.

Trying to fit new squad members into last year's system is equally unwise. Many times these new players' offensive abilities and physical build do not coincide with those qualities of the graduating seniors. Consequently, during the second year, the attack suffers. This situation does not occur in the passing-dribbling game because each participant contributes according to his specific abilities, his physical characteristics.

High school players are not, for the most part, mature enough to adjust to switching defenses. Therefore, it is mandatory that the offensive system be flexible enough to allow the defense to call the play. There are many coaches who believe that the offense dictates to the defense, but that is not true. The defense tells: a simple switch from man-to-man to a zone proves that. Success comes from not letting the defense dominate. This offensive system permits the defense to call the play and then proceeds to dominate that defense. It, therefore, has a built-in mechanism that takes ultimate advantage of switching defenses.

If the coach wants to slow down a game, there will be no adverse effect upon his team's offensive efficiency ratio. Yet the passing-dribbling game blends perfectly with the fast break *(see Chapter 10)*. By employing the passing-dribbling game, a team can control the tempo from the opening tip to the final buzzer.

Each player shoots in direct proportion to how hard he wishes to work for that shot. Therefore, it has a tendency to make the player toil harder, especially during the off-season. The passing-dribbling game is a balanced attack with each team member contributing according to his ability, and the total team receiving according to its need. Because of its demands upon the individual, each player develops more fully than under any other system.

This attack works equally well against all known defenses and it is simple, easy to teach, and easy to learn. While it is being taught, savvy is being learned. The practice time saved is enormous.

Best of all, the passing-dribbling game removes the handcuffs from the players, releasing them to be at the right place at the right time. All too often, offenses have set times for their players to move. We have seen the third cutter in a patterned offense have an advantage on his man during the first two cuts but lose that advantage by the time it is his turn to cut. Such a player and his team were handcuffed by their system, by their coach.

THEORIES OF THE PASSING-DRIBBLING GAME

A great offense must contain certain basic concepts. These axioms must be workable, and they must be fundamental. Success comes from the practical application of those postulates. All the theories discussed in this section are integral parts of the passing-dribbling game.

Follow every potential lay-up with a jump shot opportunity. There is always a vacuum behind the attempted lay-up, perfect for the jump shot.

Options can be added or deleted without serious effect upon the offense. These options should be designed to attack the weaknesses of that next opponent.

Offenses should be designed to teach savvy. Thinking and reacting to defenses are important facets of the well thought-out offense.

Modern offenses must be practicable the year around, even when the coach is not present. There are states which do not permit out-of-season practice. But with this offense the players can continue to develop on their own.

Players need to be able to free-lance; but coaches need to be able to control the offense. The passing-dribbling game can be run as a free-lance offense as well as a patterned one. If we are running it as a pattern, we do not have to reset. One option begins as the other ends, and the patterns are interchangeable *(see Chapters 7, 8, and 9)*.

Should the weakside players not be moving, and this happens some nights, the coach needs some method of mobilization. He can achieve this by reverting to pattern play.

Offenses must be adjustable during the heat of battle, the game. Not only is this offense adaptable, but the actual counters are practiced moves, which can be inverted or interchanged to occur at different intervals in the attack.

The offense must be devised to get the most from each individual's ability. And then those individual abilities must be refined into perfected team play.

Assistant coaches must be permitted to develop their own basketball ideas if the best possible program is to be achieved. Our program goes back to the third grade, and we have yet to tell even the lowest assistant what he must run. Anything he develops will blend perfectly into the passing-dribbling game.

Modern offenses must not be stoppable by scouting. Because this offense is changeable everytime down floor, it cannot be stopped by a wise scouting report.

By our rules of movement, we are checking constantly to see what defense our opponents are in. Today's defenses not only switch each time down floor, but some defenses change when the offense makes a penetrating pass, some by key words.

Offenses must be able to counter defensive adjustments. This offense not only has built in offensive team counters, but we teach individual offensive counters. Basketball is a quick moving chess game, and the team that makes the best move the quickest will checkmate its opponent.

An offense must be easy for the substitutes to fit right into. Our offense does not have positions so our players can enter into a game because they have a particular skill we need at that moment while many other offensive systems would require that the substitute know the patterns from a definite position.

Sound fundamentals must be the base upon which any offense is built. This offense is fundamental.

Any attacking system must be a foundation upon which other offenses can be added. The passing-dribbling game is the perfect base.

RULES OF ANY OFFENSIVE GAME

When we developed our offensive attack, we began by considering offensive rules that were pertinent to defeating all defenses. We proceeded to considering those rules that were peculiar only to beating man-to-man defenses, then those intended only to conquering zones. For maximum savvy, the coach should make sure that his players understand the precepts for attacking all defenses before he develops his passing-dribbling team attack.

General Rules

Floor balance and spacing are keys to attacking both the zones and the man-to-man defenses. After each shot, we require 1½ men on defense and 3½ men on the offensive boards (for offensive rebounding techniques see the sections on it throughout the book). We assign these before each game. We base these assignments on the defensive match-ups we expect from our opponents and from our knowledge of our players. On defense, we want one player at the free throw line and the other almost to midcourt. On rebounding, we want the three players to operate according to the rebounding attacks explained in Chapters 3 and 4. Regardless of who is to be the defensive safety or the offensive rebounders, we expect their positions on the court to be filled by the time the shot hits the rim.

Floor spacing is kept by requiring players to fill the holes in the particular set we are using. As one player cuts another fills his vacated spot. This not only keeps adequate space between the players, giving each player room to operate, but it permits the ball to be reversed without any delay. And reversing the ball is a most effective means of defeating sagging man-to-man and zone defenses.

All offenses, to be effective, must be continuous. We achieve this continuity by repeatedly filling vacated spaces and by constant movement on and away from the ball. When our rules are followed and our drills are run, re-run, and run again during any one possession, continuity develops.

We believe that the best offenses are those that look first to pass, then to drive, and last to shoot. We want this look and decision made instantly. We want to be looking to the goal and to be going to the goal. We want each player to dominate his defender. And although we want to pass goalward first, we do not want to force the play. Nor do we want to turn down a good shot. If we have a good shot, we want it taken; we do not want our players to look for a better one.

But we want only high percentage shots taken. High percentage shots differ for different ball players. To be high percentage, it must not be forced, it must be within the shooter's range, and it must allow us a decent change at a recovery should the shot be missed.

When the defense is man-to-man, we take the defender into a strange defensive area; and when the defense is a zone, we arrange the movement of ball and men to make the defense execute unpracticed and, if possible, complicated slides. Both of these objectives can be accomplished by movement of men and movement of the ball under the rules of Chapter 6.

Use the bounce or overhead pass from the foul line to the baseline. These are the two best passes to penetrate either a zone or a man defense.

Timing is important in attacking either the man or the zone. Proper timing is best achieved through repeated drilling. Cutters must have definite rules to govern their cutting, but they must have freedom to decide when to cut.

Best Ways to Attack a Man Defense

Both the passing and the dribbling game offenses will defeat the man defenses. If the man defense likes to sag and clog up the middle, we eliminate the sagger by switching offensive sets or by quick reversal of the ball. Switching offensive sets is also a perfect way to control double-teamers, to attack stationary zones.

However, if the man-to-man is a pressure defense, then the individual attacker should influence one direction and cut opposite, always going through toward the basket. Screening, cutting, and backdooring discourage pressure.

The offensive player should have a counter move against any defensive adjustment. This eliminates his having an off-night, and it greatly aids team offensive play. We develop these counters throughout the book, both individually and team-wise.

When the defense makes a mistake, the offense must react immediately to take advantage of the error. Several good ways to force the defense into mistakes are to post all mismatches, to change offensive alignments which make the defenders play strange positions, and to keep the defender both on and off the ball occupied.

Of course offensive rebounding is a must against man defenses. We explain our techniques in the sections on rebounding.

Penetrating the man defense with a pass or a dribble is one of our cornerstones. Our first two drills and our penetration drill introduce this aspect of team offensive basketball to our players.

Best Ways to Defeat a Zone Defense

Only the passing game is effective against a zone: dribbling aids the zone defense, giving it time to recover. But reversing the ball quickly will result in good percentage shots by penetrating the zone as it is adjusting. Under this condition, we do permit dribbling to split two defenders (see penetration drill, Chapter 3).

Playing an opposite alignment, thereby putting attackers in the holes of the zone defense, will get a quick, high percentage shot. From this set position, the offense should continuously pass, cut, and fill the vacated spots until that high percentage shot results or we get the penetrating drive with a pass off for an easy shot. Zone defenses have more trouble than man defenders covering penetrating drives because the former are not usually as well schooled as the latter on rotating tactics.

Zone offenses should stay spread, giving the zone defenders a greater area to cover. Then the cutters should constantly be looking for holes within the interior of the zone. As the ball is reversed, the zone must shift. And as the zone shifts, its interior is usually weakly defended.

The offense should keep the ball moving so that the zone will be forced to move, tiring them as well as forcing mistakes. Or the passer can fake one direction, getting the zone moving in that direction, then pass in another direction for a good percentage shot.

Overloading the zone results in many easy outside shots. Screening is also effective, especially along the baseline or in the interior of the defense.

By its very nature, every zone defense has weak spots. Those weak areas should be exploited.

But our three favorite fundamental ways are good outside shooting (this can be developed), penetrating by the pass or dribble, and getting the offensive rebound. It is easier to get the offensive rebound against a zone than it is to recover the missed shot against man-to-man.

We use all the methods described in this section to dominate both the man-to-man and the zone defenses. The passing-dribbling game, although it gives the appearance of free-styling, is organized to attack both defenses.

FOUR FUNDAMENTALS THAT MAKE A SMOOTH WORKING OFFENSE

Individual offensive techniques are an important phase of team offense. From the moment the youngster first picks up a ball, he begins learning individual maneuvers. These can be cultivated and polished by a knowledgeable coach. We show our methods of teaching this important facet of offense in Chapter 2.

Player's knowledge of attacking is paramount to having a great offensive ball club. Many opposing coaches have told us: "Johnny Player is like having a coach on the floor." We honestly try to put five playing coaches on the floor. We do this through the many drills explained throughout this book. Knowledge compensates for many shortcomings.

Conditioning is a third fundamental peculiar to all smooth working offenses. Coaches must not permit their players to remain motionless. To continue running, a la Havlicek style, requires conditioning. And conditioning should result from drills using the basketball. We never run an offensive drill without, but we are one of the best conditioned teams playing basketball *(see Chapter 10)*.

Timing is the most important aspect of team offense. It is the ingredient that separates our attack from the playground attack. Our rules (Chapter 6) and our many two and three men drills (Chapter 5) develop this all important offensive team tenet.

INITIAL DRILL OF THE PASSING GAME

The passing game offense creates team unity with free-style play, allowing only passing, no dribbling. Advocates of such a game believe that the team will miss fewer scoring opportunities, that team unity and timing will emerge through drilling, and that the individual players will develop more quickly and more completely.

Two separate offenses, one for zone and one for man, do not have to be taught. The passing game works against both.

Players can dream up many stunts on the spur of the moment to counter any defensive adjustment. It is, when mastered, the ultimate in basketball offenses.

The initial drill used to teach our system is a three-on-three half-court passing game with rules. It is an appropriate beginning drill to teach the rules and mechanics of this highly organized playground offense. In all diagrams throughout this book, 1's defender is X1, 2's is X2, etcetera, unless the offense forces the defense to switch. Then we will discuss each switch as it occurs.

Procedure (Diagram 1-1)

1. Line players up as shown. After scoring or losing the ball, the offense rotates to defense and the defense goes to the end of the line.

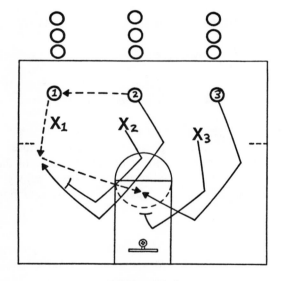

Diagram 1-1

2. There can be no dribbling, unless the attacker receives the ball while cutting for a lay-up. Then we permit a few bounces to take him to the basket.
3. The defense must play their men tight, not permitting the passing lanes to open. Coaches can, of course, change the pressure man defense to a sag or a zone. And if it is a sag or a zone, we positively allow no dribbling.
4. The offense must work the ball with passes until it scores.

5. No two cutters can break into the lane at the same time.
6. After learning to cut individually, we use the same drill to teach our screening game.

Objectives

1. To teach players to use the pass to penetrate and to score.
2. To teach defenders pressure and sagging defenses, and how to defense a cutter.
3. To teach cutters to use individual cuts as movements to score and to control the defenders away from the ball.
4. To teach passers when to use lob, overhead, and bounce passes as a means of getting the ball to the cutter.
5. To teach the attackers the first fundamental rule of the passing game: only one cutter at a time. If a second cutter sees his proposed lane already occupied, then he should use a V cut to back out.

INITIAL DRILL OF THE DRIBBLING GAME

Many coaches advocate only a passing game, feeling that dribbling eliminates the team aspect of basketball. Too often one player will do too much dribbling, but the coach should teach his players the when, the why, and the how to use the dribble. It is not the player's fault that he dribbles too much; it is the coach's.

To teach only the passing game is to teach only half an offense. We think the dribbling game has merit, especially against the various man-to-man defenses. Dribbling is a primary method of penetrating both the zone and the man-to-man. So on the first day of practice, we begin teaching a three-on-three dribbling game, which helps us to set up our rules for the dribbling game offense.

Procedure (Diagram 1-2)

1. Line players up as shown. After a score or a lost possession, rotate the offense to defense and the defense to the end of the line.
2. Before beginning this drill, the players learn the dribbling screen. It is the dribbler's responsibility to drive in the general vicinity of the cutter. The cutter is answerable to running his man into the dribbler's pick. The pass between the dribbler and the cutter should be a two-hand flip pass.
3. The dribbler does not have to pass the ball. If a defender makes a mistake, such as failure to close the gate on a switch, the dribbler can drive for the lay-up. If a switch occurs, the cutter is to clear out quickly, backdooring his new defender, and the dribbler is to reverse his direction for a driving lay-up. If the defense slides through and the offense has weaved the ball

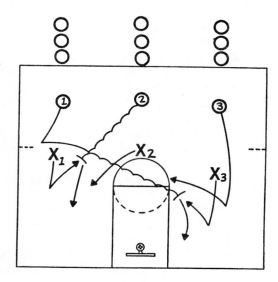

Diagram 1-2

near the basket, the cutter has the jump shot over the screen. If there is no switch after a successful screen, the cutter can drive for the lay-up.

4. The dribbler should always be in the center of the other two men, but he is not accountable to keep such a set up. It is the obligation of the other two cutters.

Objectives

1. To teach players how, why, and when to use the dribble to score.
2. To teach screening, especially the dribbling screen on a weave.
3. To teach defense to switch, slide, or fight over the top.
4. To teach the attackers the first fundamental rule of the dribbling game: always keep the dribble alive between two attackers.

THE EIGHT PASSING-DRIBBLING FORMATIONS

When coaches describe their offenses, they begin by explaining the type of personnel their offense is best suited for: for example, a quick guard, a tall forward, a good shooting corner man. What has always been perplexing to us is if the personnel on hand does not fit that mold, what good is that offense. And even if the personnel on hand does suit that offense, graduation in a few years would erode its effectiveness. Public high schools, unlike colleges and private high schools, cannot recruit personnel to fit a mold. So what every schoolboy coach needs is a system that does not depend upon specific personnel. The passing-dribbling game meets this qualification. The coach needs only five able bodies, and he is ready to teach them to play basketball.

Physical qualities and abilities are relative: they change from game to game, from team to team. One year our front line was 6'5", 6'4", 6'3", so we installed a power offense. During a tournament game, we faced 6'6", 6'5", 6'4", who could outjump us, and our power offense proved useless. We have frequently had quick teams. So we would teach, in years past, an offense to take advantage of that quickness only to run into a team somewhere along the tournament trail that was quicker.

On those nights when his offense doesn't seem to work, the defeated coach usually replies: "We were not ready tonight," "We didn't come to play," or "We were outmanned." Actually what happened, in most cases, was the coach only prepared his team for one style of play. And too often that style is too rigid to defeat a thinking team, a responsive team.

There is always a way to beat any team. That way must be found by the coach. Using these eight formations, his team attack will be versatile enough to defeat those teams that are quicker, taller, or stronger.

Some nights we are taller; some nights we are stronger; some nights we are quicker; some nights we perform with more finesse. Before preparing for each opponent, we compare their team with ours. We decide upon a course of action, one set or a sequence of sets, based upon that evaluation.

"Play your game" has become the battle cry of coaches to get their players to play the style of ball that best suits that personnel. But defeat will certainly occur when a team meets another club who is "playing the same style of game" but have better personnel. A different style of play might have won.

Coaches should sacrifice the few lay-ups of a rigid set offense in exchange for getting a season's work, yes—a lifetime's work, out of an offensive system. Many coaches who use set offenses change them two or three times a year because defenses get to know the offenses too well. The passing-dribbling game works for a season, for a lifetime; and it is the only offense that will.

The passing-dribbling game makes use of eight different sets. Some alignments are best with certain personnel (determined for that one game) while other sets work best against particular defensive ball clubs. The coach can decide on a set or a series of sets for any specific game, giving his team a distinct strategical advantage. He also has the option of running his cutting offense, his screening game, or his driving attack. A combination of two or more is also available *(see Chapter 5)*.

Because the rules are the same from all the different formations, we have chosen the single-stack set for the purpose of describing our offense *(Diagram 1-3)*. To keep explanations simple we will always let 1 and 2 be the guards, 3 and 4 be the corner men, and 5 the pivot. And when we are describing offensive

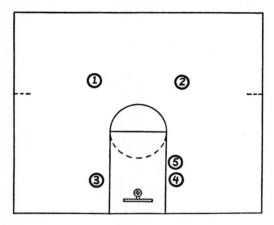

Diagram 1-3

maneuvers where size, strength, or power make a difference, we will let 1 be the smallest and 5 the largest.

While all eight formations work well against all known man-to-man and zone variations, some sets exploit certain defenses more fully than others. We will describe which alignment is better against which defense in this section. We will also explain which set works best against which defensive material.

The Single-Stack (Diagram 1-3)

If the two offensive guards are better than their defenders, hit them with this attack. If the offense has a forward who can outmaneuver his defender, this set will give maximum results. The 1-3-1, 1-2-2, and 3-2 zones can be annihilated from this formation. When the inside attackers are not quicker than their opposition but are good screeners, this attack will get many good percentage shots. This is an excellent offense when the attackers can backdoor the defenders who play denial pressure. Two inside power men can work the swing and go. Both the cutting and the driving game exploit defenders when using this set. Double-screening along the baseline makes maximum use of the single-stack.

2-3 Formation

This is the basic formation from which most high schools operate, so we shy away from using it. But we do operate from this formation when facing a 1-3-1 or 1-2-2 zone and when our pivot man is bigger than his defender. It is a good set when the pivot man is an excellent scorer and the four perimeter attackers are at least equal to their defenders in ability. And this is still the best formation to play against half-court zone presses. Cutting and driving opportunities are excellent.

This formation keeps the big center near the basket and allows inside screening for medium jumpers.

1-4 High (Diagram 1-4)

When the point guard, 1, is bigger than his defender, when the post men, 4 and 5, can operate effectively against inside pressure, or when the wing men, 2 and 3, can repeatedly drive around their defenders, many lay-up shots result from this formation. This offensive set is most productive against all zones. It is excellent against a run and jump defense, double-teaming pressure, or one that uses denial pressure. This alignment works well for good flash pivot cutters, and it is an excellent way to defeat match-up zones. Although this set limits driving, cutting opportunities are superb.

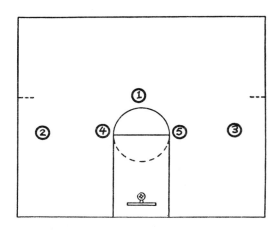

Diagram 1-4

1-4 Low (Diagram 1-5)

When the offense has an attacker, 1, who can completely dominate his defender, when the offense has two exceptional rebounders, or when the offense has two above average corner shooters, this attacking set will reap the best benefits. If, for that one specific game, the attackers can drive on their opponents, don't use this formation. This alignment gets the corner shot easily against a 1-2-2 and 1-3-1 zone. This, too, is an excellent attack against pressure from the double-teaming defenses. Flash pivot cutters can get the easy 10 feet jump shots.

The "A" Formation (Diagram 1-6)

Should the offense have a ball handler who is adept at driving his defender into a pick, the A formation is a natural. If the defense permits passes into the high post, run this formation for an easy victory. During any game where the

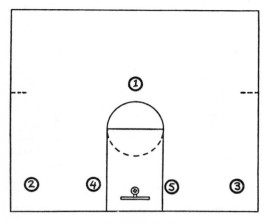

Diagram 1-5

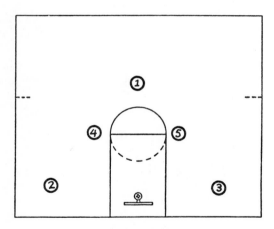

Diagram 1-6

offensive post men are better than their defenders, this offense scores easily. When the offense has a corner man who is better than his guard, lay-ups will result. This attack is equally effective against all zones, and it works well against all double-teaming defenses. If the defenders cover the flash pivots poorly, this set would get the 10 to 15 feet jumper easily. Teams that defense the screen downs poorly cannot stop this formation. Cutting along the baseline provides exceptional opportunities to score from the A.

1-2-2 Tight Or Spread (Diagrams 1-7 and 1-8)

When most of the attackers are capable of driving on their defenders, this alignment will produce lay-ups and free throws. Whenever the defense tries to

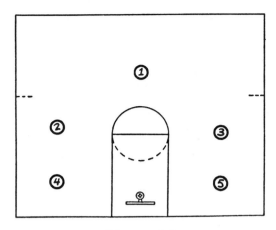

Diagram 1-7

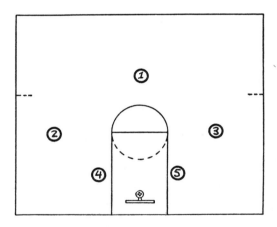

Diagram 1-8

double-team, plays denial defense, or does not sluff properly to help their team-mates, this attacking formation produces easy scores. Good cutters also enjoy success from this set. The inside screening game scores easily, especially when playing the tight alignment. This attack excels against all zone defenses, particularly the 2-3, 2-1-2, and 1-3-1 zones.

1-3-1 Formation (Diagram 1-9)

The 1-3-1 formation pays dividends against teams that cannot defense the screen down, that cannot stop the vertical rub-off, that has an exceptionally small defender. It works well when the offense has a one-on-one man capable of

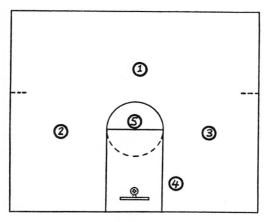

Diagram 1-9

defeating his defender a great percentage of the time. This attack is also devastating against any two-guard zone front. The set cannot be defensed by a team that uses denial pressure, run and jump pressure, or any form of double-teaming. It is an excellent offense for drivers and for cutters. A defense that permits passes into the high post area will find the 1-3-1 difficult to stop.

The Double-Stacks (Diagrams 1-10 and 1-11)

When the offense has a clear rebounding advantage, when the attackers are much slower than their defenders, when the opposition have weak inside defenders, the double-stacks might be the coach's first choice. This offensive formation permits the offense to get the ball close to the basket, especially when changing from one set to another. This alignment also works well when the defenders have trouble defensing the screen down. The coach should place his better screeners high and his better shooters low. Double-teaming or run and jump defenses will not pressure this set into mistakes. Cutting and driving are not good options from this formation, but the screening game will achieve optimum success. We do not run these alignments against the zones.

The coach must determine from game to game which set he thinks will work best against that particular opponent. He must know his players, and he must have a good idea what his opposition intends to do before he can get maximum scoring from his offense. This changes from opponent to opponent.

Before determining which set to use, the offensive coach must decide if he wishes to use his cutting, driving, or screening game. He must determine which, if any, of his players can dominate their defenders in one-on-one situations. Then the coach must determine his team quickness, size, and strength as compared to the opposition. After considering all probabilities, the coach decides on a set or a series of sets for that game.

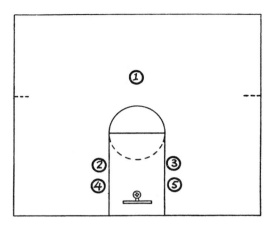

Diagram 1-10

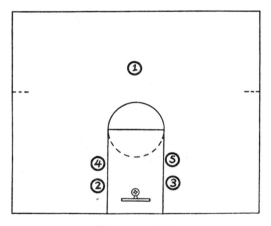

Diagram 1-11

We call our formations verbally: "Single-Stack," "Double-Stack," "13" for 1-3-1, "12 Tight" or "12 Spread" for 1-2-2, "A," "10" for 1-4 Low, "14" for 1-4 High, and "23" for 2-3. Sometimes, especially when facing a zone, we just call out different formations to get movement and a penetrating pass. We will, on occasions, run changing formations as an offense for an entire game.

A coach could, if he wishes, teach only one pattern. From the eight formations, it would look like eight different plays. We used this concept for one complete season without the opposition detecting it.

BASIC BEGINNING DRILLS USED
IN BUILDING THE OFFENSE

Many coaches take for granted that their players can move without the ball so they never drill on that activity. Instead, those coaches teach a patterned offense and let the action away from the ball occur as the pattern calls for it. But, as we have already written, rigid pattern play causes many lost scoring opportunities. We would rather drill the players on proper movement and let them pick the most opportune moment to break.

Guard-to-Guard Drills

We show each of these drills from our single-stack set; but the reader, with a little imagination, can see how the drills could be set up from any of the eight formations. During the early practice sessions, we use different alignments to teach these drills. This acquaints each player with movements from all eight formations.

Our first basic passing-dribbling game rule states that the strongside guard cuts first while the weakside guard and weakside forward interchange *(Chapter 6)*. Anytime our strongside guard cuts weakside or stands still, the weakside guard automatically runs the strongside route.

Diagram 1-12 shows the give and go cut, used when the strongside guard has a smaller man on him, when that guard is being overplayed to the inside, or when the cutter catches the defense cheating glances toward the new pass receiver, 3. When defenders away from the ball take their eyes off of their men, the attacker cuts on the blind side of his defender: that means that such a cut is a middle cut or a backdoor cut. *Diagram 1-13* exhibits the counter to the strongside give and go. We call it the pass and stand still. When 1 sees that X2 has not sluffed properly or when 2 has a smaller defender, 1 will pass to 3 and stand still. This tells 2 to become the strongside guard while 1 and 4 interchange on the weakside. We like to post small defenders low on a line of 45 with the strongside forward *(see Chapter 4)*. And these two maneuvers also give us a strongside overload with lots of offside movement against any zone defense.

Our next guard series is the pass and screen away *(Diagram 1-14)* and its counter, the pass and screen away with a roll *(Diagram 1-15)*. We run either of these maneuvers when 3 is capable of defeating his defender with one-on-one moves. 3 has more operating time before there is a cut. Both cuts, once begun, should make the defensive guards switch. Let's say that we want to post 1 on X2 we would pass and screen away with the roll. But if we wish to post 2 on X1, then we would run the pass and screen away. All of the mechanics required to perfect these maneuvers are discussed in detail in Chapter 5.

The pass and go behind *(Diagram 1-16)* sets up the most perfect two-men

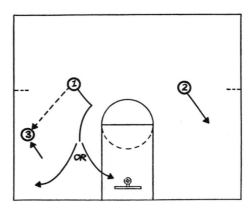

Diagram 1-12

Give and Go

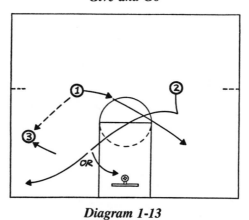

Diagram 1-13

Pass and Stand Still

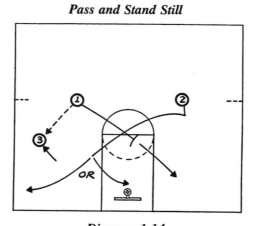

Diagram 1-14

Pass and Screen Away

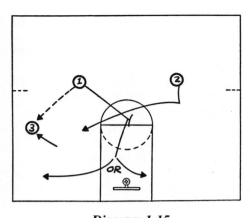

Diagram 1-15

Pass and Screen Away with Roll

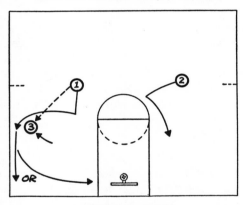

Diagram 1-16

Pass and Go Behind

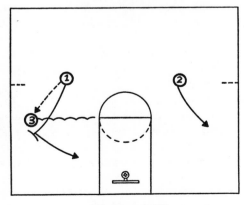

Diagram 1-17

Pass and Screen on Ball

play in basketball: the blast. The go behind also works when we want to set 3 up with a 15 feet jumper, when we want to post 3 low, when we want to switch from the passing game to the dribbling game, or when we want a screen and roll possibility between the guard and the center *(see Chapter 8)*. It has its own built-in counters, explained completely in Chapter 8.

The pass and screen on the ball *(Diagram 1-17)* is a two men play with a screen followed by a roll. It should be used when 1 has a weak defender or a small one, and 3 is an exceptional one-on-one player.

We begin these drills on the first day of practice, teaching the players their initial movement from our rules offense. They learn early that they must decide what to run and when to run it. We spend a great deal of time on how to run it. Who said savvy can't be taught: we just did.

Unless we are inverting our offense, we begin our plays with the strongside guard option. But when we invert the rules, this would be the last part play of our offense.

To teach these maneuvers, the coach should have his players form three lines, one each behind 1, 2, and 3. The lines should rotate so that each person could run each spot. We switch spots from practice to practice so that they will conform to the eight basic sets. At first the cuts are run with no defense. But after mastering the when's, the why's, and the how's of cutting, we add the defenders and correct the mistakes made by the players in their choice of cuts.

Guard-to-Forward Drills

We run the pop out or post low option *(Diagram 1-18)* when the defense permits 3 to shoot over the screen or when 3 is taller than his defender. Frequently we will have 3 screen for 1, getting X1 on 3's back and then post 3 low, especially when 3 can out operate his defender along the baseline low post position.

The V cut or flash pivot *(Diagram 1-19)* is run anytime 3 is quicker than his defender. We also run this when the defense fronts our center on the strong side. From this same position we run our blast series (explained in the next section and in Chapter 5).

Our center calls our second option by his choice. And one of his choices is to head hunt on the weakside. So we use a drill where 3 cuts off a screen by 5 for a quick jump shot *(Diagram 1-20)*.

Another guard to forward drill we use concerns the penetrating pass *(Diagram 1-21)*, and we like to drill on it against live defensive pressure. It, too, is a V cut. However, this cut is away from the scoring area. A completed pass to 3 as he moves outside keys 1 to run his options: strongside cuts, weakside cuts, or the go behind. If overplayed with too much pressure, 3 backdoors his defender for a lay-up.

The forward to guard screen *(Diagram 1-22)* is an entry into the offense without a pass to the cornerman. We run this when we have difficulty completing

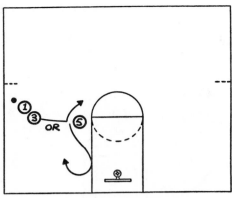

Diagram 1-18

Pop Out or Post Low

Diagram 1-19

The V Cut or Flash Pivot

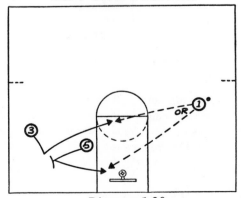

Diagram 1-20

Cut Off Center's Head Hunt Screen

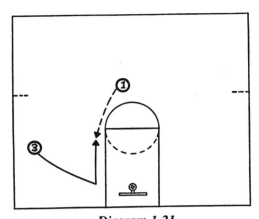

Diagram 1-21

V Cut Versus Denial Pressure

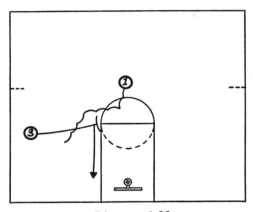

Diagram 1-22

Forward Screen for Guard

the penetrating pass. It is also an excellent maneuver when 1 has a small defender on him and 3 has inside posting capabilities.

Unlike guard to guard drills, we always run these cuts with active defense. It is a waste of time not to require pressure defense, using the pressure to teach the savvy involved by correcting wrong decisions.

Perimeter-to-Center Drills

We label these drills perimeter to center; but, in fact, they can be perimeter to forward drills *(see Chapter 5)*. These five maneuvers help to develop the blast, the greatest two-men offensive play in basketball. We show these maneuvers

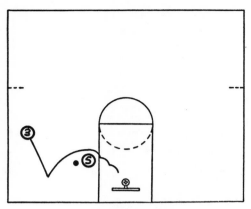

Diagram 1-23

Hand-off Drive

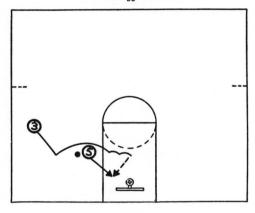

Diagram 1-24

Screen and Roll

from the forward position, but they can be performed by a guard-forward or guard-center combination.

After completing the pass inside, and there are many ways to make this pass inside *(see Chapter 4)*, the outside attacker dips and comes off 5's inside baseline hip *(see Chapter 5*, the section on the blast for the pivoting mechanics). Our first maneuver is to hand the ball to 3 and let him drive for a lay-up *(Diagram 1-23)*. We run this option when 3 has run his man into the pick set by 5, and X5 has not switched.

The screen and roll option *(Diagram 1-24)* is a counter to X5 switching after 5 has made a mistake by handing 3 the ball. 5 should have X3 on his back and should be open for a pass from 3 for a power lay-up.

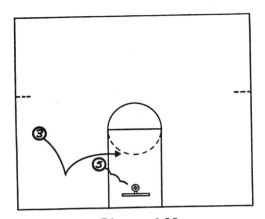

Diagram 1-25

Pivot, Fakes, Blasts

Diagram 1-26

Delayed Pass

Diagram 1-25 displays the correct option for 5 when X5 switches to 3. 5 should keep the ball and take one dribble for a blast lay-up. X3 would be on 5's back and X5 would be with 3.

Frequently X5 will stay with 5, and 5 will only partially pick X3. When this happens, 3 should continue to the bucket for a delayed pass and a lay-up *(Diagram 1-26)*. Because X3 was partially picked, he must race to recover on 3. 3's hard cut goalward should leave him open temporarily.

Many times the defensive man on 3 will go behind 5's pick *(Diagram 1-27)*. When this happens, 3 should have the easy 10' jumper over 5's screen.

We run this drill every day during our early practice sessions. We begin with no defense, then we add X3, and finally we add X5. Although in later

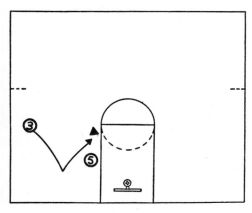

Diagram 1-27

Shot Over Screen

practices we allow 5 to work one-on-one inside, and this option is always availa-ble, it is a bad policy to permit 5 his individual moves too early. 5 would constantly be looking for his one-on-one moves instead of allowing the pattern to develop fully.

FORWARD RUB-OFF DRILL

After teaching the above options, we run the forward rub-off drill, which teaches the attacker with the defender to make correct decisions. The drill, explained below, has X1 as the defender; but X5 is another possibility. We do not begin with both defenders; we progress from using X1 to using X5 to using both.

Procedure (Diagram 1-28)

1. Rotate players from 1 to X1 to 5 (to X5 if he is in the play) to end of the line.
2. 1 must run X1 into pick being set by 5.
3. When 1 has rubbed off X1, he may jump shoot or drive for the lay-up. If overplayed in direction of the pick, 1 can backdoor his defender or 1 can double-fake change of direction for backdoor or set up pick.
4. Sometimes we employ an X5 to help jam-up the situation and to help 5 consider his options. When this happens, 1 and 5 may pick and roll or blast.
5. Sometimes we do not use a defender. Under that condition, it is just a shooting drill with 1 jump shooting over a screen or 1 using the option dictated by the coach and by 5's choices.

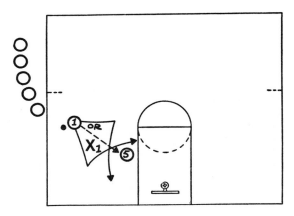

Diagram 1-28

Objectives

1. To teach 1 to run his man into a screen.
2. To teach 1 when to jump shoot and when to drive.
3. To teach X1 proper fighting over a screen.
4. To teach 5 the proper method of a flip pass.
5. To teach X5 proper defense and 5 proper choices when he has a defender.
6. To teach the blasting options *(see Chapter 5)*.

CHAPTER 2

Developing Índividual Moves
for the Passing-Dribbling Game

Five individuals working separately will never play championship basketball; five fully developed, confident players working cohesively will, year after year, win the ultimate championship. But before a coach can enlarge into team play, he must be sure that each individual is capable of recognizing how to defeat his defender. Teaching the attacker when to use which individual cut or maneuver is of primary importance to the passing-dribbling game. The why is obvious.

It is the coach's job to develop these (why, when, and how) instincts in his squad. Team offense can never be any stronger than its weakest individual performer.

STRENGTHENING THE ATHLETE

While defenders need to be quicker than their attackers, offensive players need to be stronger. They need to be stronger physically and mentally.

Books have been written on how to develop the athlete physically. We do not think any scheme is appreciably better than any other. It is only important that the player begin a program and stay with it. However, there is that thin line of demarcation where improvement in physical strength begins to diminish quickness. The coach must recognize that saturation point, different with each player, and release his physically improved player from that program.

Mental development is at least equal to physical development. The athlete must be told repeatedly to be mentally tough. There are those who will try constantly to derail their own express train of improvement. If the future offensive star expects to achieve, he must constantly overcome his adversary and his many obstacles. His greatest adversary will be himself, and his toughest obstacles will be in his own mind. Super stars are mentally tough. And although every player that we get will not become a super star, it must be the goal of each.

REVERSE AND FRONT PIVOT DRILLS

Reverse and front pivots are bases for many maneuvers in the passing-dribbling game offense. The dribbling crossover, for example, makes use of the front pivot; the dribbling reverse makes use of the reverse pivot. Many of our cutting techniques, at some point, involve a deep knowledge of these pivots.

So we teach them early. And then we refer to the pivots by name when we want them used in a maneuver.

The individual pivot drill teaches the mechanics. The team pivot drill exposes the when and the why.

Procedure (Diagram 2-1)

1. Line players up as shown. Rotate from front of line to back.
2. 1 dribbles to the coach who checks the player's pivot carefully.

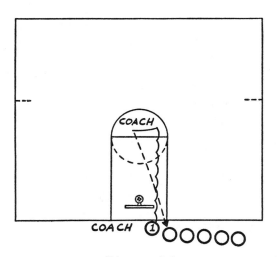

Diagram 2-1

3. If the coach wants a front pivot, 1 begins by jump stopping, using his left foot as the pivot foot, bringing his right foot between himself and the foul line coach, turning his back on the foul line coach. 1 passes to next man in the line who dribbles to the foul line and front pivots. The next time through the drill we have the players use their right foot as the pivot foot.
4. If we are teaching the reverse pivot, we have the player to jump stop, use his left foot as a pivot foot, swing his right foot between himself and the

baseline coach, turning his back on the foul line coach. He passes to the next man in the line and the new dribbler reverse pivots. On the next trip we have the players use their right foot as the pivot foot.

Objectives

1. To teach the front and reverse pivots.
2. To teach pass coach wants (pass back to man in line).
3. To teach protective dribbling.

Now we teach the when and the why. When: to maneuver away from the overplay, to protect the ball from defenders, to commence an offensive move as in the buttonhooks, and many, many more maneuvers explained throughout the book. Why: to get away for the defender. The player can escape after pivoting by using the dribble or the pass. When an attacker cuts without the ball, he can use either or both pivots to gain a strategically advantageous position between his defender and the ball.

Team Pivot Drill

Procedure (Diagram 2-2)

1. Line players up as shown. As 1 drives into the center, 5 overplays him, and 1 reacts by using either the front or reverse pivot (whichever the coach wants), passing to the first man in the line in the direction he pivots.

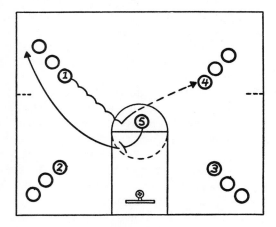

Diagram 2-2

2. The defender goes to the end of the dribbler's line.
3. The dribbler-pivoter becomes the new defender.
4. The man receiving the pass becomes the new dribbler-pivoter.

5. After the players have progressed sufficiently, the coach can add another ball to expedite the drill.

Objectives

1. To teach the when and why of the two pivots.
2. To teach the idea of the defensive overplay.
3. To teach protective dribbling and passing.

After learning the basics of pivoting, we review them daily in a drill that takes only one and one-half minutes. We divide the squad into groups of three. We give one player the ball, and we put the other two on defense. The two defenders try to steal the ball as the ball handler pivots to protect it. Each player handles the ball without a dribble for thirty seconds. This drill also teaches the defenders how to force the held ball and how to double-team. It teaches the attacker how to split his defenders by use of proper pivots.

SECRETS TO MOVING WITHOUT THE BASKETBALL

We have one basic rule that governs our movement without the basketball: When a player starts a cut and sees a teammate cutting, the second cutter makes a V cut back out. This eliminates two attackers from congregating near the scoring area by cutting to the same spot at about the same time. We repeatedly emphasize that it is far better to cut late than to come too early.

But regardless of practice time spent trying to limit the number of cutters into the same area, two or three players inevitably end their cuts at about the same spot at least a few times each game. We have learned to turn that to our advantage. When two or three cutters gather at the same spot, we require that those players cut in two or three different directions and that the man with the ball hit the first open cutter with an overhead pass.

The man with the ball calls the break by slapping the ball with both hands, much as he would call an out of bounds play. As the cutters break, their movement screens the defense, making it easy to get a pass inside to at least one of them. The cutters who do not receive the ball clearout if the defense is man-to-man and cut backdoor if it is a zone. We have found that such a congregation of cutters is a blessing in disguise when used sparingly. But there is a need for a warning: If a player is not in a position to receive the ball while cutting, he should immediately clearout or screen for a teammate.

There are three essential ways of scoring against both the zone and the man-to-man defenses: an individual maneuver, a screening offense, and a cutting attack. The cutting game is as successful as the other two, but few teams make optimum use of it against a man-to-man defense. All teams use cutting as a basic tenet against the zone defenses.

Cutting can be made more effective by allowing the cutter to choose his moment of cut. The famed third option of the Auburn Shuffle, for example, has the weakside forward making a V cut and becoming a side post man. His cut comes after a guard has run a lateral rub-off, and the center has broken around a guard screen. Now a smart defender knows the V cut is next and he will be prepared to stop it. Wouldn't the V cut have been more successful if the weakside forward could cut at his pleasure? And his pleasure should be at the slightest defensive mistake. Cheating a glance toward the ball, sagging too far to help on a free cutter, turning the back on either the attacker or the ball are all examples of defensive mistakes. And at the exact moment of the mistake, the cutter should break to the ball for an easy score. That is one of the major advantages of the passing-dribbling game over the set patterned attack.

Our players learn many cuts. We drill on these cuts until every player has mastered them. We teach the when, the why, and the how. It does not take long for the players to instinctively recognize which cut to use and why. But don't take for granted that the players know how to cut or when to cut; they must be taught.

Dip

The dip, a simple V cut, is used primarily to free a cutter from his defender for a pass so that a play can be continued. The cutter steps toward the basket so that his defender must give ground. Then at the most opportune moment, the attacker plants his outside foot, pivots on it, and comes back toward the ball to receive a pass. We prefer for the cutter to receive the pass with a jump stop (discussed later in this section) because this enables him to pivot in any of four directions which we feel are necessary for the most effective inside offense (see section on triple-threat position).

Middle Cut

This cut is run whenever any attacker feels he can get his defender on his back *(Diagram 2-3)*. The defender must make a mistake in order for the attacker to achieve this advantage. A simple pass to the middle cutter results in a lay-up and most probably a three-point play. Diagram 2-3 shows the middle cut from the corner and from out front. Both cutters, of course, would not be breaking at the same time. If the defender is playing excellent defense, the cutter can aid his cause by faking in a direction away from the ball, planting his outside foot, and quickly changing his direction toward the ball for a successful middle cut.

The Give and Go

Frequently a passer's defender will watch the flight of the pass. When this happens, the attacker can cut between his defender and the ball for a return pass. Another frequent defensive mistake made by a passer's defender involves the

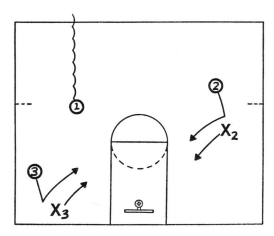

Diagram 2-3

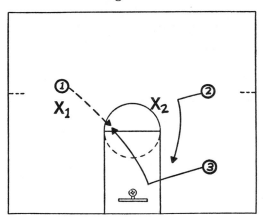

Diagram 2-4

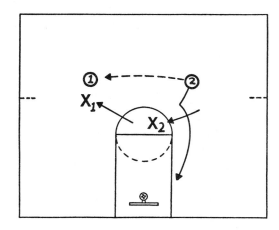

Diagram 2-5

slowness in the defensive jump toward the pass receiver. Under that condition, the passer should immediately break between his defender and the ball. The give and go is a pass followed by a middle cut.

Backdoor Cut

Diagram 2-4 illustrates a backdoor cut without a preceding pass by the cutter. 3 runs a dip followed by a flash pivot cut. 1 hits 3 as 2 influences X2 toward 3. If X2 reacts by watching the pass to 3 or by stepping toward 3, 2 will plant his outside foot and change his direction, backdooring his man for a pass and a lay-up. If X2 does not sag toward 3, 2 will cut around 3 for the blast *(see Chapter 5)*.

Diagram 2-5 discloses a backdoor cut off a pass. Should 2 pass to 1 and X2 sag in the direction of the pass, 2 should influence a few steps inside and break backdoor. This prevents teams from sagging and eliminating the middle cut. Also, upon receiving the ball, 1 could drive toward X2, forcing X2 to hedge and hesitate, allowing 2 to backdoor X2, or permitting 2 to position himself for a pass from the driving 1 for an easy jump shot.

We use both of these drills in our early practice sessions. They help to teach our cutters to cut and our defenders to defend.

Flash Pivot Cuts

We have two drills which we use to develop the flash pivot cutters. This is the area where we would most like to get the ball. Many different attacking cuts originate from the flash pivot area: the blast, individual cutters, one-on-one, off-side screens, splitting the post, to name a few. Although our diagrams show the cutter coming from the corner, it can be a backcourt cut or even the center spinning or pivoting. We prefer for it to be someone who has a size advantage on his defender.

The cut is a break across the lane area, using a dip, change of direction, spin, reverse pivot, or whatever maneuver is required to get the defender on the flash pivot's back (see Chapter 4 for more explanation on the spin and reverse pivot). We always want to be moving toward the ball when receiving the pass from 1. *Diagram 2-6* shows the dip toward the basket and the change of direction back toward the ball. *Diagram 2-7* depicts the double change of direction and movement back toward the ball. We rotate position of 1, 3, and X3 until we are sure that all members of our squad have learned to be a flash pivot cutter from the corner and from out front.

Rub-Off Cuts

Rub-off action usually takes place away from the ball. *Diagram 2-8* exhibits 1 running X1 into 5's pick. If X1 goes below 5, 1 comes over the top for a pass from 3 and a jumper. If X1 goes over the top of 5, 1 breaks low for a pass and a lay-up. 5 does not move, nor does he attempt to screen. 5 stands still, allowing 1

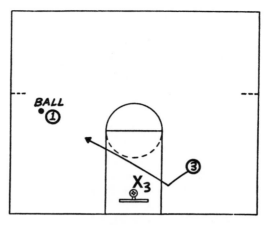

Diagram 2-6

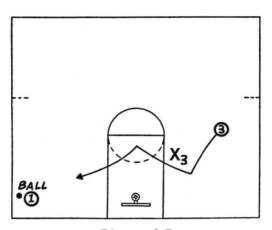

Diagram 2-7

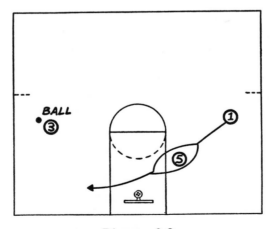

Diagram 2-8

to change his direction, dip, or use any move needed to rub X1 off on 5. The success of the maneuver rests exclusively with the cutter, 1, and how well he can maneuver his defender. If X1 anticipates 1's rub-off cut and sags into the free throw lane area as 3 receives the ball, 5 sets a front screen on X1, reverse pivoting in the direction X1 chooses to run back toward 1 as 3 throws an overhead crosscourt pass to 1 for the jumper.

Change of Direction

To make this cut, the attacker influences in one direction, plants his outside foot, then breaks in yet another direction. We teach it in a mass drill, having all players race toward a coach. The coach changes direction of the cutters by jumping to cover on the other side of a chair. When the players reach the end line, usually after two or three change of directions, another coach brings them back to the other end line, again changing directions by jumping to an opposite side of chair. We like visual commands because basketball is played by visual reaction.

Change of Pace

We use the same mass drill to teach the change of pace. The players begin running at full speed toward a coach. When the coach raises his hand, the players slow down. When he drops his hand, the attackers speed up again.

We combine the change of pace and change of direction into a third drill. Using the same mass drill and the same visual commands, the players learn to change pace and change directions interchangeably. These are musts in developing movement away from the balll, in controlling the weakside defenders, and in freeing the weakside attacker for a pass.

Double-Fake Change of Direction

Diagram 2-7 demonstrates the double-fake change of direction. Of course, the attacker could change directions three, four, or more times during any possession. If he keeps running and changing pace and direction, he will at least keep his man busy and out of the play, possibly freeing himself for an easy shot.

We teach the change of direction, change of pace, combination of the two, and double-fake change of direction from the first practice session. They not only teach our players to have continuous motion with a purpose, but they help in early season conditioning.

The Buttonhooks

Before we can develop the buttonhook, we teach the front pivot and the reverse pivot (earlier in this chapter). The straight buttonhook makes use of the front pivot; the buttonhook with a pinch uses the reverse pivot.

The straight buttonhook is run whenever the defender is ahead of the cutter.

If the defender, X3, is higher but ahead of the cutter, 3, as in *Diagram 2-9*, 3 would front pivot off his left foot. This puts X3 on his back and enables us to get a pass to 3 inside. From this position, we could run the perimeter to center drill *(Chapter 1, diagrams 1-23 through 1-27)*, we could post 3, forming the line of 45 *(see Chapter 4)*, or we could run the go behind *(see Chapter 8)*. If the defender is on the baseline side of 3 but ahead of him, 3 would front pivot on his right foot and again establish position with X3 on his back.

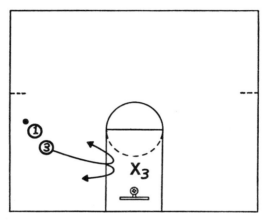

Diagram 2-9

Should X3 trail 3, we would reverse pivot buttonhook with a pinching move. If X3 is higher than 3 and trailing him, 3 would stop, reverse pivot on his left foot, swinging his right foot completely between X3 and the baseline. Now a lob pass goalward by 1 would give 3 the lay-up. If X3 is trailing 3 low, then the reverse pivot would be on his right foot, swinging his left foot between X3 and the foul line. A lead bounce pass thrown toward the foul line sets up the perimeter to center drills, the blast, or the go behind.

Stride Stop

We teach this maneuver by using the same mass drill as we used for the change of direction. The players are required to race downcourt until they see the coach raise his hand. Then they must stop with the back foot as their pivot foot and their forward foot several feet in front. To do this their buttocks must be low. When executed properly at great speeds, this drill will develop better offensive balance for the players.

Forwards, played by denial defense, use the stride stop to free themselves for a pass and for a backdoor cut. This stop enables the attacker to use the foot closer to the basket as his pivot foot, and he has his forward foot to help secure the pass and keep his defender from stealing it. Denial defense played too closely results in a foul, and when continued too far outside results in the backdoor cut.

Jump Stop

Pivot men make best use of the jump stop. The jump stop is a must in setting up the blast. We teach it initially by the same mass drill described above. When the coach gives the running players the hand signal to stop, they jump forward, landing on both feet simultaneously (now they have two pivot feet). To accomplish this while running at great speeds, their center of gravity must be low, their buttocks must be low, their elbows should be out to the side, and their hands should be underneath their chins. If the players had a ball in their hands they would be ready to pivot either direction and begin an individual move or a team play. The reader can easily see how we can progress this mass drill into pivots and one-on-one play.

SECRETS OF THE TRIPLE-THREAT POSITION

Positioning of the various parts of the body are identical to the jump stop position. The lower legs should be perpendicular to the floor. The knee joint must be 135 degrees or less. The angle at the midsection should be 135 degrees or less. The elbows should be extended outward about letter high or lower. The hands should be in front of the letters, cupping the ball. All offensive movement, with or without the ball, originates and ends in this body position.

From this triple-threat position an attacker is ready to pass, drive, or shoot with a minimum of movement. Consequently, the act is quicker. And this is exactly the order in which we want the attacker to consider his options: pass, drive, or shoot.

To be able to pass effectively and most efficiently, the passer must keep the distance between himself and the receiver at a minimum. Passers do not make any unnecessary movements: they use fakes only for a purpose. Passers should see the passing lane and the receiver without looking at them. The pass must be made to the receiver's open side, the side away from the defender. There is an exact moment when the receiver is most open, and at that moment the pass must be delivered. When the pass is made, pass it—don't baby it.

Passers should ignore flat-footed receivers. Should a player pass to an immovable target, it would be the passer's fault if there were an interception.

Should the receiver have his back to the basket, after receiving a pass at all inside positions except the low post, we want him to immediately pivot into a triple-threat position, facing the basket. We teach three such pivots.

Diagram 2-10 shows the pivot we use when we are maneuvering to set up a teammate. We pivot on the left foot because it enables us to get out of the three second lane without using the dribble. However, we use the pivot of *Diagram*

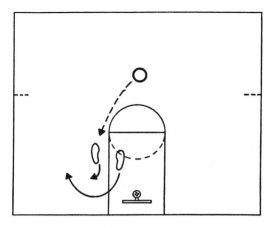

Diagram 2-10

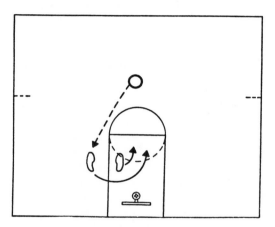

Diagram 2-11

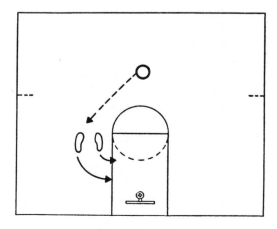

Diagram 2-12

2-11 when we expect to go one-on-one. The reason is simple: it puts us about five feet closer to the basket, and we are going to move quickly for the score.

We use *Diagram 2-12* when we are running the blast option. It is a pivot on the right foot as in Diagram 2-11, but this time we only pivot half-way, perpendicular to the baseline. If the pass had been made from the corner and we were running the blast, we would use the pivot of Diagram 2-10. This enables us to set a perfect back pick on the cutter (explained more fully in Chapter 5). This pivot is not really triple-threat position; however, we include it here so that all pivots used by players with the ball inside will be covered at one time.

SECRETS TO ATTACKING ONE-ON-ONE

From the triple-threat position, an attacker can pass, setting up other players, or he can attack one-on-one. In other words, he is ready to drive or to shoot.

Offensive men are to attack the front foot of their guards, whether they intend to drive or to shoot. This is the most vulnerable foot of the defender. If the guard plays with a parallel stance, attackers will either shoot (because parallel stances require playing some distance from the ball handler) or they will force the defender to choose a front foot by placing the non-pivot attacking foot beside one of the parallel feet of the defender.

The only other way an individual attacker can be defended is by an over-play. We have individual moves in our dribble series to defeat this defensive tactic. We also have a team method of attacking the overplay *(see Chapter 3)*.

One-on-one players must know when to fake. All coaches have witnessed a player faking after receiving a pass within shooting range with no defender on him. Or the attacker will wait until he is approached, and then he will begin faking. We contend that such a player should shoot as he receives this pass because he is in what we call the near perfect position: having the ball inside his scoring range with no defender on him. This situation occurs many more times than the coach imagines, especially when playing against a zone or a sagging man-to-man.

One-on-one players must learn not to over fake. They must avoid unnecessary movements. Often a player can fake one direction and continue that direction for an easy shot.

When practicing a fake, the player should keep stepping backward and forward until the fake becomes a smooth, fluid, rhymatic motion. Just as a good writer reworks his material, changing small segments until it is polished, the good faker will perfect his moves, changing those portions of it to correspond with his physical and mental development until it is faultless.

However, when a defender plays an attacker tightly, he must have individual moves if he is to escape. And we have certain guidelines to make those one-on-one moves more effective. We like for the fake to be a natural movement.

A fake should be related to a move used previously during a game. This gives the fake an air of reality. We design our fakes to force the defender to look into the attacker's eyes, to look at the ball, or to get into motion.

Once begun the drive should be in a straight line (if not, the defense will recover). We do not want any herky-jerky motion.

When a player defeats his defender with any of the following moves, he should score on a lay-up. But some defenders can recover sufficiently to regain decent defensive positioning. When that happens, the attacker should change his direction, preferably by the crossover or behind the back move, at the exact moment the defender recovers, and he should settle for the jump shot.

For every attacking move, we want a counter move developed. Should the defense adjust to the first move, the counter would be employed to defeat the adjustment.

Whether the attacker has the ball or is moving without it, the fake must be made toward the defensive man. The closer we get to the defender, the harder it will be for him to cover our next sudden move. This forces the defender to make a decision. And once we get the defender to moving, we have him whipped.

Attackers must develop mental toughness. Even if he is stopped time after time, he must muster up the courage to try and try again. After repeating the one-on-one drills innumerable times, the player will begin to sense the precise moment he has his defender at a disadvantage and the best technique to use in completing his drive or shot.

To win at one-on-one, the attacker must defeat the defender with his mind and his feet. The offense must work at this; he must think every situation through; and he must perfect our basic dribble and drive series (explained next). To these series, the attacker may add any sequence of moves he likes. We say sequence because one fake will not do: it must have a counter move. One-on-one players must learn to maneuver from the fake and drive position before they begin considering the dribble series.

SECRETS TO MOVING WITH THE BASKETBALL

Fake And Drive Series

Learning to execute the fake and drive series helps us show our players the evils of the one bounce habit. To quickly bounce the ball or begin the dribble series is to limit their attacking ability to one-half: They no longer have the fake and drive half. It is logical, therefore, that the fake and drive series be taught first. And we teach all of these maneuvers from a one-on-one drill position. We give the attackers the ball at the foul line. Attackers are within shooting range, and the coaches have a line from which they can better judge their player's expertise.

X Ball Fakes

Eyes are an important part of the fake shot-drive maneuvers. The players should be looking at the basket, giving the impression of shooting.

A lot of coaches do not believe that ball fakes around the perimeter are very effective. We always try to receive the ball within shooting range. Then we use two sets of ball fakes around the perimeter. We teach three ball movements from the triple-threat position: long; long, short; long, long, short. A long ball fake indicates that the shooter brings the ball from the shooting pocket to a position over his head; but while executing a short fake, the attacker would stop the ball at about eye level. These movements should be real shooting attempts or real dribbling attempts. The slightest movement of the ball goalward will often cause the defender to become off-balance, creating the easy drive for the shot. The second set does not begin from triple-threat position. We hold the ball with both hands down low, swinging the ball from one side to the other. The slightest movement of the ball in a lateral motion will often cause the defender to adjust for the dribble, creating the easy drive in an opposite direction. If we catch the defender watching the ball, and they all do at times, he is very susceptible to a drive. If we do not get the guard off-balance with either of the first two series of fakes, we bring the ball back to triple-threat position and move to our next series of fakes.

We coordinate these ball fakes with head feints, giving an impression of leaving our feet for the jump shot. If none of these moves are successful, we move to the foot fakes.

Jab Steps

Most offensive players move too fast. Patience must be developed. After getting the defense off-balance, the attacker wants to move quickly and he wants to use a long first step. But while faking, the offensive players should move moderately quick, always maintaining perfect balance. The jab step, besides being a great fake, will teach this.

For discussion purposes, we will use the left foot as the pivot foot, and we will let the defender's forward foot be his left foot.

In attacking, we should move our right foot with several short stutter steps toward and outside the defender's left foot. If he does not give ground, we drive. If he gives ground, we jump shoot or use our rocker step.

Rocker Step

If we have extended ourselves a few stutter steps and we are unable to drive because the defense is not off-balance, we will quickly pull our feet back almost to normal position, pretending to shoot, but keeping our balance forward. A fake shot move will help get the defense to rock forward. If the defense reacts to this rocker movement by coming forward to stop our shot, we will take a long step toward the front foot of the defense for a drive and a lay-up.

The shooter must not return completely to normal position because that would force him to shift his center of gravity back to the center of his original base. And the advantage of the rocker step is the offense has his center of gravity forward while the defense is shifting from center of base to a forward center of gravity. A sudden burst goalward while the defense is reacting forward will get the lay-up.

Fake One Direction-Drive That Direction

This is the basic move off the rocker step. It is run when the defense does not react to the fake in a particular direction or when the defense overreacts by reacting then returning to normal position. The drive takes courage and must be executed quickly. The driver should rub his shoulder by the defender as he explodes goalward.

Fake One Direction-Drive Opposite

This requires an offensive crossover step, and that is a slow move. If the attacker is quicker than his defender, he will not need this move. It should be run when the attacker finds the defender's front foot beside his pivot foot or when the defender is in a parallel stance. This move will get the defense in motion, and that motion leads to a defensive mistake. We group this maneuver with our drive and jumper from the dribble series which creates many individual opportunities.

Half-Step Jumper

When we began playing front foot to pivot foot defensive stagger, it became obvious that we needed a new offensive move to defeat that defensive stance. Therefore, the half-step jumper was invented. Let's say that the defender's right foot is forward (*Diagram 2-13*), and we are using our left foot as pivot foot. A fake right would not move the defense, but it might cause him to place a little weight backward. When we see this defensive mistake, we immediately jump shoot. The jump does not have to be high, but it must be quick. We adjust while in the air. The shot is taken from the waist up, using the legs for upward explosive power, creating no off-balance feeling. This shot can become amazingly accurate with practice. We combine this move with what we call the drive and jumper to make a perfect sequence to attack front foot to pivot foot defenders.

Twister

This is the counter to the half-step jumper and the crossover. Bill Foster invented the twister while at Rutgers. As the attacker takes the half-step toward

Diagram 2-13

the defender's back foot, he also tries to give the impression of leaning in the opposite direction, but he keeps his pressure on his pivot foot. Should the defense lean to stop the fake one direction-drive opposite, we push off on a straight drive. Should the defender lean to stop the fake one direction-drive that direction feint, we crossover and drive opposite. When mastered, this is a most effective counter to the half-step jumper and to the crossover.

Dribble Series

After teaching the fake and drive series, we begin to teach the dribble series. These two series must be taught in this order. After receiving a pass, many young players want to immediately put the ball on the floor. If they are made to fake and drive before dribbling, they quickly learn the disadvantage of the instant bounce habit. And they will have a full offensive faking system instead of one-half: just the dribble series.

Straight Drive

Usually it is sufficient to simply put the ball on the floor and drive directly toward the basket, rubbing shoulders with the defender. We caution our players never to look for a better shot if a good one is available.

Up and Under Drive

Many times, especially when being approached by a weakside man-to-man defender or by any zone defender, a fake shot and drive under is sufficient to get penetration. The attacker must be able to drive both left and right; he must be able to shoot lay-ups even off the wrong foot; and he must be able to pull up short and take a middle range jumper. Drilling perfects the how and when of all of these maneuvers.

Crossover

We use a one line drill to teach the mechanics of this all-important dribbling move. We run it down the right sideline, then the left sideline with no defense. Then we place the attacker on the foul line with a defender. The attacker cannot get out of the lane, and he must use the dribbling crossover to get a lay-up.

The attacker drives, let's say down the right side of the court, until he is cut off, then he changes direction by planting his outside (right) foot forward, quickly bringing his inside foot forward, crossing the ball in front of him, and swinging his right foot forward again, protecting the ball with his body. When the attacker plants his outside foot, he should also give an outside head and shoulder fake. When he brings the ball back in front of himself, he should take it as low as he can and as quickly as he can.

Reverse

We use the same two drills that we used in the crossover, except this time we require the dribbling reverse. Players dribble down the right side of the floor until they are overplayed, then they stop on their outside foot (right), plant their inside foot (left), reverse pivot on their left foot, controlling the ball with their right hand until they have completely changed directions (*Diagram 2-14*). To switch hands too early would leave the ball out where it can be stolen. Once they have changed directions, they switch dribbling hands, using their bodies to help protect the ball. Switching hands too early also results in many palming violations.

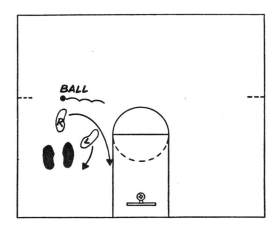

Diagram 2-14

We run the crossover whenever we are subject to being double-teamed. Otherwise we would run the reverse or the behind the back dribble because they offer better protection of the ball.

Drive and Jumper

This is the most effective move in basketball. We stress it. We run this as another counter to the front foot to pivot foot staggered stance. Let's say the defense has his right foot forward and our left foot is our pivot foot. We put our right foot cross the defender's right foot, take a long dribble, and jump shoot. This maneuver works because the defender must give ground with his front foot on our crossover or we will drive all the way. The move must be made quickly, and it must be practiced along with the regular jumpers to become a high percentage shot.

Drive All the Way

We use this maneuver anytime the defense will allow it. Its threat helps our other fakes. The coach should require his players to drive all the way and shoot in all kinds of body contortions, including using the wrong foot. A well-padded broomstick could serve to throw the driver off-balance and help to create game-like contact situations.

Stop and Go

This is used to get the defender moving and to get him off-balance. The attacker dribbles hard and fast, then he stride stops, leaning backward, but keeping his weight on his forward foot. When the defense relaxes or leans forward, the attacker pushes off and explodes goalward.

Behind the Back

A short time ago, only show-offs used the jump shot. All coaches frowned upon such a shooting technique. Today, the conservative coaches will call the behind the back dribble ''hot-dogging.'' But it is the easiest and safest way to teach the change of direction dribble with almost no chance to lose the ball, and the dribbler does not have to turn his back on his defender. The ball is kept between the attacker's body and his defender, making it impossible for the ball to be stolen. The attacker does not turn his back, making it harder for the defense to double-team him. And the attacker can keep the whole offensive court in his field of vision, making it easier to hit the open man.

Dribble Drop Step

The attacker dribbles with his body protecting the ball, using shuffle steps, never crossing his feet. When the defense cuts the dribble off, which must happen or the defense concedes the lay-up, the attacker reverse pivots on his front foot, swinging his back foot completely in front of the defender's trail foot *(Diagram 2-15)*. Now an explosive dribbling reverse gives the offense the inside route to the basket. As he reverses, the attacker should also use his elbow to hook his defender. The move should be slowly calculated; the attacker can try to maneuver his defender into an overplay for five seconds without violation of the rules.

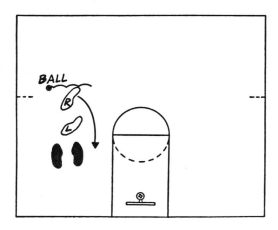

Diagram 2-15

Fade Away Jumper

Smaller players, who do not jump well, need a move that allows them to get their shot off against taller defenders. The fade away jumper is such a maneuver. The shooter, however, must jump directly away from the bucket, not to one side. It is easy to compensate for the distance, and the percentage reaches the straight jump shot potential when practiced diligently. Having never had tall players, we have resorted to practicing and developing the fade away.

Twisting Jumper

Instead of a fade away, which comes directly at the end of a drive, the twisting jumper offers an opportunity to catch a taller defender off guard. The player drives, picks up his dribble, pivots 180 degrees, putting his back to the basket. Now it is hard for the defender to picture a jump shot from this position, so the twisting jumper is a surprise move. But that is what the attacker does: he twists in the air, squaring his shoulders before releasing the shot. And when coupled with the fade away jumper, the twisting jumper will get the attacker two free throws. How? At the end of the drive, the 180 degree pivot will look like the fade away jumper. And after fading away a few times, the defender will jump toward the attacker to stop the fade away. The shooter usually gets fouled as he is twisting in the air.

SUMMARY

Armed with these maneuvers, every member of the squad can take advantage of every scoring opportunity that comes his way. Attackers can add to their repertoire by divising still more counters to defensive adjustments. Some players will become advanced enough to learn many more sequences of fakes (a fake and its counters).

The fakes in this chapter deal exclusively with facing the basket. We require that our big men know these fakes as well as those described in the chapter on big man play. We also require that our small men learn the big man fakes. In the passing-dribbling game one is never sure who will be playing inside and who will be playing outside.

Players must learn to take their best shots, especially when the chips are down. Too often this is when players take their poorest shot, one that is often unpracticed. We like to give the attacker the ball at midcourt and give him five seconds to score. This not only teaches our players poise in trying situations, but it helps us in taking the last shot of each quarter.

One-on-one basketball will not win championships, but a team cannot be completely competent until all its players are capable of ultimate contributions. We spend considerable time teaching and practicing these maneuvers. As our players improve, we add sequences. The players can drill to perfect them on the playgrounds during the off months.

Coaches take for granted the development of moves. But unless those coaches have super-stars year after year, they will not be consistent winners. Unless they have a program of fakes, and have drills to implement them, their offense will not be great year after year. Our offense stresses pass, drive, and shoot in that order so we must be well versed in individual attacking moves.

Players must learn to shoot from a standing or faking position as well as off the dribble. The only way the shooting percentage will rise is by practice, practice, practice. But practice will not always make perfect. Players who work long and hard and make little or no progress cannot be blamed for getting discouraged. Players under those conditions are not shooting a fundamental shot. The coach should teach the techniques correctly; then when shooting is practiced, players will improve. Outstanding and unique shooting drills are offered in Chapter 3.

CHAPTER 3

Coaching the Perimeter Attack
for the Passing-Dribbling Game

Without the fundamental shot of basketball, the outside shot, there can be no effective inside game. Getting the ball down court is a prerequisite to setting it up. A quarterback must learn ball handling and savvy before patterns can become an accomplished and successful team technique. In fact, there have been few, if any, super teams without great guards. And not every high school or college has a good big man around whom an offense can be built. But every coach has a group of small men waiting to learn to become super players.

GENERAL REQUIREMENTS FROM THE PERIMETER POSITION

Guards have the primary responsibility of calling the formation that will best dismantle and unnerve the defense. After calling the set, the guards must decide on the first cut unless we have inverted the offense. Defense dictates that first cut and it should result, if possible, in an advantage for the offense. We believe in getting a shot off the first move every time down the floor. We do not want to miss any conceivable scoring opportunity.

Coaches should scout their opposition, and the several practices prior to playing that opponent should be spent preparing the guards for their potential calls. Using the knowledge in Chapter 1, any coach can prepare any guard to recognize which set and which option to run.

This position has no size requirements nor are speed and quickness prerequisites. Coaches must drill their backcourt men to be brilliant in their selections. And to help the coach tutor his protegé is one of the purposes of this book.

So the coach must develop his guard's expertise. Players must be informed and drilled in all the available options. They must mentally master Chapter 2 and the last half of this chapter.

COACHING THE PERIMETER ATTACK 65

Cornermen occupy the other perimeter positions. They begin the passing-dribbling game by receiving the ball, watching their teammates cut and maneuver; therefore, the forwards must read what their teammates are doing and react accordingly. They also can make the first one-on-one moves.

Cornermen also do not have any size or quickness requirements. They, too, just have to have savvy.

Because we run from eight different alignments, it is sometimes difficult to determine who runs as a guard and who runs as a cornerman. We try to place these men in the positions where they will do the offense the most good. The guard, other than the point guard, would usually play a wing. The tallest cornerman is generally moved inside on the 1-4, 1-2-2, and 1-3-1 formations. But there are no hard set rules. Coaches will have to evaluate their material and make wise assignments based on those assessments.

However, we have rules for our players to assume certain positions should the fast break be unsuccessful. The first two players down floor are the guards, the next two are the cornermen, and the last player down floor is the post. If we are running from a point offense, the first player into the offensive end of the court is the point, the next two are wings, and the last two play inside. If there is no fast break, the last two players across the time line are the guards. This gives us different players playing different positions each possession, thereby giving the offense incredible versatility and explosive beginning power (see Chapter 10 for what happens when the fast break is unsuccessful).

But this is a detail that the coach will not have to pay close attention to. Players gravitate toward a natural position for them. A coach might occasionally have to decide who plays where when there is no fast break.

BASIC STRATEGY FROM A BACKCOURT POSITION

In the passing-dribbling game, the backcourt position does not necessarily mean a guard. All players have to be able to play all positions. The backcourt position is occupied by the first two men down the floor after an unsuccessful fast break or by the last two men down floor when there is no fast break. Not only does this give us extra versatility in our offense, but it compels defenders to play different positions on different possessions. Too often, defenders race downfloor to a specific area and wait on the attacker. That cannot be done in the passing-dribbling game. And occasionally we get an easy bucket while a defender is trying to find his attacker.

Coaches decide strategy, but the quarterbacks must know what to call and when to call it. And the coach should always explain why. In fact, modern players demand to know why.

When facing a team that likes to double-team or run and jump, we run a point offense. This requires the double-teamer to run an extended distance to set the double-team, and an accurate pass to the spot just vacated by the defender can easily result in penetration. And penetration will result in a lay-up or a high percentage shot.

But we do not run a point attack when their defender is capable of controlling and dominating our point man. This will be a rare situation. But if the defense has an exceptional point defender, we run a two guard front.

We start each game with a two guard front unless we are sure of our opponent's defense. Although it is easier to stunt from a two guard defensive front, it is also easier to attack; and in the case of an exceptional defender, we can decoy him more from a two guard front without losing any offensive punch.

However, a sagging man-to-man defense will bring us out of our two guard backcourt combination. In that case we send the weakside guard through to baseline corner on the weakside. This clears out the sagger, forcing the sinking man-to-man to play us straight.

SECRETS OF DEVELOPING THE LITTLE MAN

Little men have one conspicuous advantage over big men: they can move their feet and bodies quicker. Wise coaches of talented little men will exploit this superiority.

To be successful in today's fast paced game, the little man must have superior quickness. Little men generally possess quickness because of their body make-up, but there are drills which will add to anyone's quickness.

Strength is the first thing to look for. If the athlete has weak legs, build them through a weight lifting program; if he has weak arms, build them through isometrics. There is that thin line of diminishing returns when an athlete's strength begins to diminish his quickness. But up to that line, his quickness will increase directly with his strength.

Playing one-on-one against last year's quicker players will build quickness. The coach can develop the first guard by sending him to a summer camp where quickness is a premium.

We allow our guards to shoot from twenty feet. In fact we insist upon it. To develop a shooting touch from that distance requires a great deal of practice. We insist upon that. Every year our opposition and the newspapers applaud our guards: "Powell Valley always has such great shooting guards." We develop them, and their development does not happen in one year (see section on "touch.")

Besides shooting from outside, we teach our guards ball handling. We use the Globetrotter Drills along with a few we devise to meet a particular guard's peculiarities. So add shooting to ball handling, and the sum will be a great driving guard. And we teach our guard to drive and pass off by using our penetration drill. Savvy, the ingredient that makes a mediocre player great, is taught by the material enclosed in this book.

SECRETS TO DEVELOPING TOUCH

It is said that some of our shots sprout legs and climb into the basket. Outside players must be able to shoot and the better ones shoot with touch. Developing the illusive touch will not occur overnight. It comes only after long hours of diligent preparation.

We never let a player come onto the court and begin shooting. His first shooting act should be within a few feet of the backboard. The player should shoot the ball and let it hit the backboard with backspin. The player should check his wrist flip and keep his elbow in, lifting his shot in the process. Does the ball come off the middle finger is a question that must be answered affirmatively. Twenty such shots daily should suffice.

The shooter then moves in front of the rim, only a foot away from the goal. He jump shoots, but his shot cannot touch iron; it must hit only twine. The shooter steps back one step and jump shoots again. If he hits the rim, he must stay at that spot until he hits only net. Upon hitting only nylon, he steps back another yard. After moving out five steps, he goes to one side of the goal and repeats the process. After successfully hitting from five yards back, he goes to the other side of the goal. After a few years, the player becomes so proficient that we graduate him to a side goal which has a shooting ring on it. Shooters are developed, not born.

Before a player can go to the showers after practice, we require that he hit a jump shot from nine positions: they differ with different players. Players are at first allowed to miss any two such shots. By the end of the season, they must hit nine in a row. The coach should choose the nine shooting spots to correspond with the player's shooting spots during a game. The little man should have at least one or two attempts from twenty feet.

Although shooting is inately fun and athletes do it without persuasion, the enjoyment derived from shooting can be increased by devising competitive shooting games. We make use of about one hundred different drill games. Competition spices up free shooting during the off-season. It becomes difficult to keep the players out of the gym.

PENETRATION DRILL

The greatest individual play in basketball is not a beautiful one-on-one move. It is an offensive player driving by his man, another defender picking him up, and as this other defender picks him up, the driver passing to the open teammate for a lay-up. Coaches praise this play, but they spend little or no time developing it, taking for granted that the good player can do it and the poor ones never will. The penetration drill instills mastery of this play in all our players.

Procedure (Diagram 3-1)

1. Line players up as shown, in a line at midcourt. Rotate the players from 1 to 2 to X2 to X3 to 3 to end of the line.
2. 1 drives to the basket while X2 covers 2 and X3 covers 3, simulating 1 driving past his man.
3. At first the coach, who is behind 1, signals which defender is to pick up 1. 1 immediately lays the ball off to that open man for a lay-up.
4. After running the drill a few days, we permit the defenders to rotate in any direction they desire. This makes 1 have to find the open man in a rotating man-to-man or zone defense.
5. From practice to practice we change the beginning area. Changing areas simulates splitting zone defenders. And after several practices we assign X1 to 1. And after X1 lets 1 beat him, X1 rotates to help out X2 or X3.

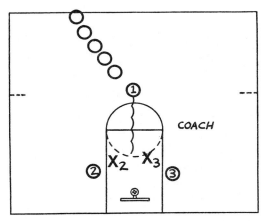

Diagram 3-1

Objectives

1. To teach the lost art of driving.
2. To teach passing off a drive.
3. To teach the inside men to shoot the power lay-up.
4. To teach the driver to develop various types of controlled passes and shots off the interrupted drive.
5. To teach defenders to rotate and help out on the open man.

But before driving, an attacker should know how much of his path is uncontested and whether the defense is zone or man-to-man. If the defense is a zone, a perimeter driver can expect to be cut off before reaching the basket, and his teammates should cut to the spot vacated by the defender. If the defense is a man-to-man, the driver should be alert for a defender to rotate to him. The teammate who was covered by the rotator should race backdoor if the other defenders do not sink and should break behind the driver for a pass and a jump shot if the other defenders do sink. This enables the driver and his teammates to know when to stop for the jump shot and when to drive and pass off. This aids the driver in finding the open man and assists his teammates in breaking to the right spot for a pass or in anticipating the rebound. A drive, therefore, does not have to terminate as a lay-up.

Drivers must constantly be evaluating and re-evaluating the defense that is in front of them. Two men closing fast means a double-team so the driver should halt the dribble and pass to a teammate. A driver who has beaten his defender can continue until the defender gets help, then the driver should lay the ball off to his open teammate. If a defender is in an overplay position, the driver should reverse for the jump shot.

The driving stance is the same as all the other offensive basketball stances. It is especially important that the eyes be up, seeing the location of all the offensive players and how their defenders are playing them. The most important defenders to notice are the potential defensive helpers. Their stance will inform the driver where he can expect to be cut off.

Speed is not as important as proper execution of the fakes of Chapter 2. Good feints will get the drive started; the penetration drill will end it successfully.

SECRETS OF A GUARD ATTACKING
HIS DEFENDER'S OVERPLAY

Modern man-to-man defenses channel attackers in pre-determined directions by means of an overplay. Individually our players overcome this defensive tactic by reversing directions, but most defensive coaches teach their defenders either to scramble back into an overplay on the other side or to use defensive team trapping tactics. So we have resorted recently to teaching an offensive team technique that frustrates and often conquers the overplay. This maneuver forces defenders to play attackers head to head.

Let's say that 1 is bringing the ball up the floor and X1 has been told to cut him to the outside where the defensive team will double-team or put into effect some defensive team maneuver. 1 quickly picks up his dribble *(Diagram 3-2)* and passes to 3. 1 does not hesitate even a moment but cuts hard toward the basket shielding X1 by keeping his body between the ball and X1. 1's first step must be with the foot that is on the side of his defender. This will always put X1 on his back. A lead bounce pass gets 1 the inside power lay-up. X1 cannot recover because of his poor initial position (overplay to the inside). All other players are cleared to the weakside of the court so X1 has no defensive help.

Let's say that X1 has been told to cut 1 inside where there is help (a most

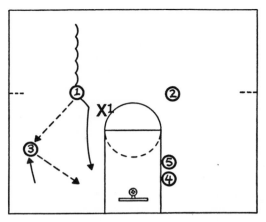

Diagram 3-2

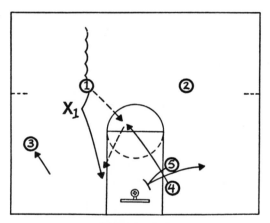

Diagram 3-3

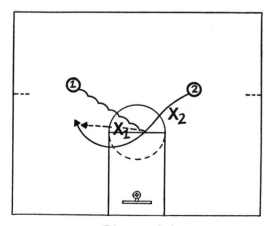

Diagram 3-4

widely used defensive overplay tactic). 4 must read this if the offense is to take advantage of X1's proper overplay *(Diagram 3-3)*. 1 passes to 4, who has used 5 as a screener, and 1 again breaks goalward, keeping X1 on his back. 4 immediately throws a lead bounce pass to 1 who has the inside track to the goal for the lay-up. 5's clearout for the possible pass and a five foot jumper compels X5 to go with him.

These maneuvers must be drilled upon so that 1's move is instant and so that proper team timing can be achieved. Any delay on 1's part would permit X1 to scramble back into excellent defensive position. Forcing the team defense out of their overplaying stunts illustrates how we allow the defense to dictate what to run offensively and then we dominate that defensive decision by turning their dictates into a defensive mistake. Impelling head to head coverage also gives us better faking and driving opportunities.

The option does not have to start from a guard position. An overplayed forward can initiate it.

SECRETS OF FREEING ONESELF
FROM DENIAL PRESSURE

Overplayed weakside guards often stand still and beg for a pass, especially if the strongside guard has lost his dribble. There is absolutely no way to get the ball to such a player. Consequently passing stops, off-side movement ends, the offense suffers. Weakside guards learn five tactics to rid themselves of their denial defenders.

Many times a simple dip, two or three steps toward the basket with a quick return out front, will get the weakside guard open. Most players, however, do not dip suitably or this option would always work, negating any need for another. We use a string to teach our players the proper dipping procedure. Imagine a string stretched tight between the attacker and his defender. To dip correctly this string must be relaxed. Getting the string relaxed requires the invader to get close to his guard so that it would be impossible for the defender to cover the attacker's next sudden move.

If the weakside dip does not work, the weakside guard goes behind the strongside guard on a dribbling exchange. When the defense is double-teaming any cross of the ball, we do not use this option. And when the strongside guard has picked up his dribble, naturally this option would not be available.

Instead of going behind the strongside guard, who is dribbling toward the weakside, we could loop in front of him *(Diagram 3-4)*. When the strongside guard has lost his dribble, looping is still effective. The weakside guard would middle cut and then loop to a wing position. During this maneuver the two cornermen should be exchanging sides or at least timing their dips to free themselves for a pass inside.

A fourth freeing maneuver is the backdoor cut or the middle cut. The defender dictates which. If the cutter uses the backdoor cut, the weakside corner should have already cleared out his area. If the cutter uses the middle cut, he still has the option of going baseline or looping.

When these fail, we have the weakside guard screen the weakside forward. This screen, aided by a good dip and a quick break by the cornerman, should clear the horizontal pass to the breaking forward. But should the defender still overplay the forward, a poor team defensive stratagem, the cornerman has the perfect angle for backdooring his defender. In order to backdoor successfully, the weakside guard, after screening, must clear quickly to the baseline strongside.

SECRETS TO DELIVERING THE BACKDOOR OPTION

Besides using the fundamental passes of basketball, the passing-dribbling game insists upon three: the backdoor bounce pass, the high lob pass, and the overhead posting pass. All three passes receive extensive coverage in this text.

Before players learn the backdoor bounce pass, they master the cut. The backdoor cut is more successful when the weakside is cleared. As the backdoor cutter takes his three or four steps goalward, the passer begins dribbling toward the cutter. Upon seeing these two maneuvers, the weakside cornerman and post man clearout. When the backdoor cutter plants his outside foot to break outside, he must have his mind made to either backdoor or come outside for a pass. If it is the backdoor cut, he only takes one step outside. And as the defender shifts his weight to deny outside, the backdoor cutter plants his inside foot, breaking hard off of it toward the basket.

As the passer sees the first step goalward by the backdoor cutter, he throws a bounce pass that strikes the floor underneath the defenders arm. The cutter, realizing that the pass will be at the defender's feet, cuts a step further away from his defender than ordinary. That way the ball bounces up to waist level. And the deeper cut allows the receiver a fraction of a second longer to see the ball, eliminating the bobbled pass.

The Backdoor Pass Drill

Many coaches take for granted that players can complete this play. By substituting the backdoor pass drill for the daily lay-up drill, the coach can improve the execution of the backdoor option.

Procedure (Diagram 3-5)

1. Line players up as shown. 1 rotates to X1 to 3 to X3 to end of the line.
2. 1 dribbles toward weakside while 3 is setting up X3. X3 knows what is coming and offers only token resistance as does X1. X3 exaggerates his step outside just before 3's backdoor cut. Use of two balls keeps the drill snappy.

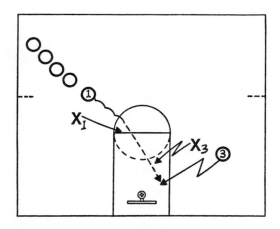

Diagram 3-5

3. 1 delivers the bounce pass at the precise moment. The coach should switch directions and positions on the court from day to day.
4. X3 gets the rebound and passes out to next man in the line.

Objectives

1. To teach the backdoor pass and the backdoor cut.
2. To teach receiving backdoor pass for a lay-up.
3. To help teach denial defense.
4. To effect timing, a basic tenet of all successful team offenses.

SECRETS OF DELIVERING THE LOB PASS OPTION

If the backdoor option is not apparent, perhaps the lob pass option will be. The backdoor cutter could continue to the opposite side, then break back into the flash pivot area for the lob pass. We also like to run this option from the strongside when our low post man is fronted and the ball is in a line of 45 *(see Chapters 6-10)*.

A weakside lob pass option from the Overload set *(Chapter 7)* is shown in *Diagram 3-6*. 5 has a smaller man, X2, on him and he is the only player on the weakside. We could pass into the corner to 3 or inside to 4 or reverse the action to 2. But when badly mismatched on the weakside we want 5 to become a flash pivot cutter. When X2 cuts him off, as all good defenders are taught to do, we want the pass lobbed into the air slightly longer than the goal but not on the backboard. X2 probably would turn his back on 1 as he cuts 5 off. This is the moment to pass the ball, letting 5 run under it. 5 has perfect position to go high

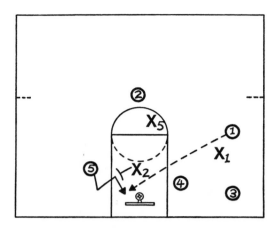

Diagram 3-6

into the air over X2 and lay the ball in. This is a dual purpose drill. It not only teaches X2 proper flash pivot defense, but it enables us to get work done on our lob pass option. But the primary drill used to teach the lob pass is shown in *Diagram 3-7*.

Lob Pass Drill

Procedure (Diagram 3-7)

1. Line up in two lines as shown. Rotate to end of other line.
2. 1 throws high lob pass to 3. 3 catches and lays the ball in goal. 1 rebounds. This drill is substituted for lay-up drills, and we change areas of the court frequently.

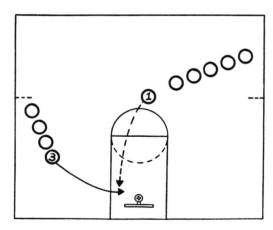

Diagram 3-7

3. To deliver a perfect lob pass, 1 must have both hands on the ball in triple threat position. He flips his wrist as in a two hand set shot. He keeps his eyes focused on an area about a foot from the rim.

Objectives

1. To teach the lob pass techniques.
2. To teach 3 to catch ball and shoot concurrently.
3. To help develop coordination to use the lob pass.

Opportunities to use the lob pass are presented in Chapters 7, 8, 9, and 10. Players master the fundamentals first.

SECRETS OF THE SPLIT THE POST SERIES

By our rules, presented in Chapter 6, centers work one-on-one immediately after receiving inside passes. Perimeter cutters must learn to recognize if the center has this one-on-one advantage. If the one-on-one superiority is not apparent, the next option is to split the post.

Proper passing-dribbling game procedure for the splitting series calls for the passer to cut first. The second cutter has many options: he may split using the first cutter as a screen; he may fake split and go down the same side as the first cutter; he may head-hunt, screening for someone else to complete the splitting series; or he may run the blast if the center has not dribbled. Backcourt men must know both the first and the second cutters' responsibilities. They will be called upon to be both *(see Chapter 4)*.

Although the first cutter can blast, middle cut, pass and go away, and the many other options available to him, for discussion's sake let's let him begin by splitting the post (see later section this chapter for first cutter's options). The second cutter, who is usually the guard because we like for our pivot passes to come from the side, reads the first cutter's options and chooses his best option. If the second cutter splits the post, it is a sign that his defender has played him straight and the first cutter has set an adequate screen. The second cutter should either get the jumper over the screen or a flip pass for a driving lay-up. If the second cutter fake splits, it is a signal that his defender has overplayed the split or the two defenders are switching and waiting on the cutters. Either way a back-door cut and bounce pass gets the lay-up (see section on backdoor cut). The second cutter's third option is to head hunt. This frequently happens when a pass has been made into a high post man with the low post occupied. It should result in the man being screened getting at least a jump shot over the screen. This option gets the two weakside men into the split, and they should have been exchanging (by the rules outlined in Chapter 6). The last option by the second cutter is a delayed cut. To run this option the second cutter must wait until the first cutter has cleared strongside.

The blast, explained in Chapter 5, is the best of all the inside two man plays, and it should be considered first by the delayed cutter. This delayed cutter can backdoor, screen for the center and roll, or let the center run a dribbling screen. If none of these options are available, the center finds an open outside weakside man for a pass and a jumper or beginning of a new pattern.

Only the backcourt, or second cutter's responsibility, has been discussed in this section. The first cutter and the center's duties will be discussed later in this chapter and in Chapter 4. Chapter 4 will also show all the options of the split the post series.

We teach these options by a three-on-three drill *(Diagram 3-8)*. We drill on these options until every man is instinctly aware of and continually make the correct decision. Diagram 3-8 illustrates a pass inside from cornerman, 3, after 1 cut to strongside corner. This is the first move from the overload formation *(see Chapter 7)*.

Split The Post Drill

Procedure (Diagram 3-8)

1. Line players up as shown. Rotate from 1 to X1 to 3 to X3 to 5 to X5.
2. X3 is first cutter and must split the post.
3. If we want to run 1's third option, we add a few offensive men on the weakside.
4. Sometimes we go five-on-five with only the splitting series being available.

Objectives

1. To teach all the options of the splitting series.
2. To teach jump shooting over the screen.

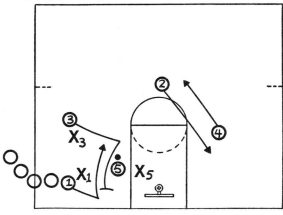

Diagram 3-8

3. To teach the blast.
4. To teach the flip pass for the driving lay-up.

SECRET REBOUNDING ATTACKS
FROM THE WEAKSIDE

Tall guards offer excellent opportunities to send four offensive men to the boards; quick guards are the best players to send to the free throw line for the long rebound. We send at least three and one-half men to the boards. We violate this rule only when facing a team that does not fast break. In that case, we send a fourth man: the tall guard if we have one.

Rebounders are assigned from the beginning of the game. The short and long safety are also assigned, and we expect these men to assume their positions regardless of where they are when the ball is shot. That gives us definite responsibility with no delay, and we would have our best men in their best positions. When the coach has a fine rebounding guard, it is best to send him to the boards because it is a most difficult task to block him off.

When our tall guard rebounds better than a forward, we send the guard to the board and the forward to short safety at the free throw line. When neither guard is an exceptional rebounder, we send the quicker guard to the foul line.

This short safety, whether guard or forward, has averaged better than three baskets per game off long rebounds or "garbage." Most games are won or lost by less margins. It is a most important rebounding position.

We arm our rebounders with as much knowledge as experience and research has taught us concerning how the ball usually caroms. Rebounds ricochet to the opposite side from which they are shot more often than not. This also happens to be the area where boxing out is the most difficult to accomplish, especially if the weakside is continually moving.

But some teams screen out all the offensive rebounders effectively. When the opposition is keeping us from this vital rebounding area, we clearout as the shot is being taken, letting another teammate try for this positioning. We accomplish this in several ways.

First we let the weakside cornerman move to the foul line while the point guard races toward the baseline weakside rebounding position. If this is not successful, we have the cornerman screen for the point guard as he moves toward the baseline. And, lastly, we let the cornerman roll after the successful screen for the point guard.

We only run these maneuvers against man-to-man box-outs because zone teams use triangular rebounding. Against the zone teams, we anticipate the shot by knowing the peculiarities of our players and our offensive system, and this expectancy gives us a head start for rebounding position inside the defensive triangle.

SECRETS OF ATTACKING PRESSURE

Defensive teams use a variety of stunts and tactics aimed at forcing an offense out of its attack. It is difficult to ascertain the passing-dribbling attack much less pressure the offense out of it. But some teams try.

When faced with individual pressure, our guards go directly toward it and attack it. We teach three methods: crossover dribble, reverse dribble, and the behind the back dribble *(Chapter 2)*. The drill we use to attack individual pressure is the full court zig zag *(Diagram 3-9)*.

Procedure (Diagram 3-9)

1. Line players up as shown. The attacker dribbles down the floor and back then alternates with his defender.
2. Coach should begin the year by telling dribblers which move to use. The defense must force at least three changes of direction in each half-court.
3. All action must occur within one-third of the court's width.

Objectives

1. To teach dribblers to attack by crossover, reverse, and behind the back dribbles.
2. To teach defense to dictate direction by means of an overplay.
3. To improve ball handling.

When faced with team pressure, the backcourt men must recognize the type of pressure. If it is man-to-man or run and jump, we clear out. If the team pressure is a zone press, we use the team maneuvers that are described by guard to guard, guard to forward, and guard to center sections in this book. We also post our big men at various intervals down the floor. We run our rule game, described in Chapter 6, and our full court passing game drill *(Chapter 10)*.

SECRETS TO AVOIDING THE DOUBLE-TEAM

Guards must be alert. Modern day basketball presents a variety of double-teaming methods. Vigilant guards can detect these defenses unfolding. Having full and proper vision of the court, therefore, is a key to avoiding traps. So the reverse dribble must never be used when expecting a double-team.

To escape the double-team, teamwork must be instituted. To attack a man-to-man double-teaming defense, such as run and jump, the player whose defender is applying the double-team returns to receive a pass. If another defender has been employed to shoot the gap, then the attacker who had been guarded by the gap shooter returns to receive an outlet pass. To escape the zone press, we employ our rules of Chapter 6 and the full court passing game drill.

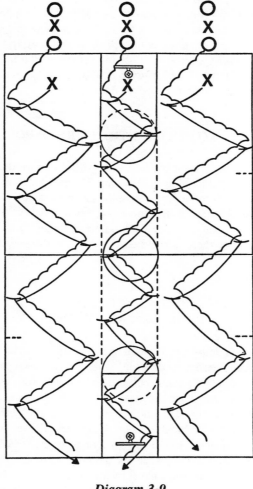

Diagram 3-9

Gap shooters provide the offense with an excellent free throw opportunity. All pass receivers should be moving toward the passer as they receive the ball. Any contact with a defender who is attempting to steal the pass will result in a defensive foul. The burden for absence of contact rests more with the defense.

SECRETS OF GUARD'S POSTING THE MISMATCHES

When we have a guard who is taller than an opposition defender, we like to post him low. If the smaller defensive man has been assigned to the taller attacking guard, we pass to the forward and run a give and go or middle cut. If the smaller defender has been assigned to a smaller attacking guard, we have the taller guard, 1, pass to 3 and go screen for 2. After screening, 1 rolls to the basket *(Diagram 1-15)*, setting up at a low post position and putting into operation our posting mechanics *(see Chapter 4)*. 1 should set the screen higher than normal, forcing X2 to go behind 1. A quick reverse pivot would prevent X2 from getting back to 2, making the smaller X2 cover the taller 1.

SECRETS TO PLAYING THE CORNER POSITION

Cornermen are important to the passing-dribbling game, not so much in initiating action as in being able to read and respond to the inaugural cut. They must be able to shoot from medium range, be adequate rebounders, and above all continuous cutters. Cutting is the most important function of the cornermen. They must cut to get open; they must cut to post; and they may cut to operate on a weak defender. All of these cornermen cuts will be discussed in the next four sections.

SECRETS OF FREEING ONESELF
FROM DENIAL DEFENSE

There is no trouble getting the ball to a cornerman when facing a zone or a passive man defense. Difficulty develops when the defense uses denial pressure. So we developed counters for our cornermen to use to free themselves.

Counter number one is the dip, and it should begin as the guard is bringing the ball across the time line. This move can be countered by the backdoor cut if pressure is still tight on the break outside. If neither of these two maneuvers are productive, the strongside forward can go screen for the weakside forward who can break to the strongside for a pass. We also like this interchanging of position when we want to post our weakside forward low.

Our last individual counter calls for the cornerman to go to the baseline about five feet in from the corner. While there he reads his defensive man. If the defender shades the attacker on the baseline side, a simple reverse pivot would put the defender on the cornerman's back. If the guard remains in complete denial, the cornerman takes the defender to the spot where the guard no longer can see both the attacker and the ball. If the defender holds the cutter, it is a foul. If he closes to the ball, the dummy play is a lay-up. If he opens, the attacker makes sure that the defender loses contact, and the cornerman either loops above the defender or the forward front pivots on his inside foot, putting the defender on his back before breaking outside for the pass. Or the cornerman may choose to post low if he has an exaggerated mismatch.

SECRETS OF TAKING UP THE SLACK

Many defenders take the middle ground: pseudo-denial and quasi-sluff. Those defenders think this puts the offense about twenty feet from the basket, and each defender still can offer help inside. So we have developed offensive team counters that not only combat the semi-sluff, half-denial, but enable us to score off the first pass.

The attacker's first move is directly toward his defender. He gets as close as the defender will allow, forcing the guard to play defense or concede the lay-up. When the defender decides to play the attacker, his defense must be denial or behind. If the defense stays low, the attacker reverse pivots, running the middle cut. If the defense plays high, the cornerman fakes outside one step and runs the backdoor; or if the attacker has a size advantage, he would run the lob pass option. If the defense continues to play even, the cornerman reverse pivots low, getting inside position to the basket. When the guard sees this, he brings the ball into a line of 45, setting up the posting position described below and in Chapter 4.

SECRETS OF THE LINE OF 45 OPTION

Because the passing-dribbilng game advocates posting all exaggerated mismatches, setting up the line of 45 is a major responsibility of the cornerman. By the rules of this system, the guard passes to the forward and cuts. The center cuts next. These cuts are designed to get the ball into a low post position. And we have our outside man, in this case the cornerman, set up the line of 45.

During all our games and practices, we have discovered that it is nearly impossible to prevent an inside pass to a low post position if the attackers are in a line of 45. The line of 45 means that a line through the passer and the receiver will meet the baseline in a 45 degree angle.

It is obvious that if both attackers were permitted to move we could search forever for the 45 degree line. So we make it the responsibility of the outside man. It is easier for the perimeter ball handler to maneuver, and he is in a better position to visualize the 45 degree angle. That strategy also leaves the inside player to concentrate exclusively on receiving the pass and scoring.

SECRETS OF CORNERMEN'S POSTING THE MISMATCH

Strongside cornermen can post low immediately by taking up the slack as described above. They can also post by the backcourt men calling the go behind. Weakside cornermen can post by letting the strongside screen the weakside man's defender. Of course, we only run this option when the weakside attacker is taller than the strongside defender. If the weakside cornerman is taller than his defender, we would post him by a low flash pivot cut.

Cornermen who have a size advantage can break to the low post strongside position anytime they wish. Their only restriction would be our rule of only one cutter at a time. The art of posting is discussed fully at beginning of Chapter 4.

SECRETS OF THE SPLITTING THE POST SERIES

Cornermen, in our offense, make the inside pass. Centers then have the first option of going one-on-one. Strongside cornermen must consider the center's option before beginning the splitting series. Others involved in the split time their moves by the cornerman's movement. In Chapter 4 we will discuss in detail the splitting and fake splitting possibilities.

After his initial splitting cut, the cornerman must set a screen for the second cutter. If the screen has been set well enough to cause a defensive switch, and if the cornerman's defender is on the same side of the center, then it should be easy for the forward to roll to the goal with inside position.

The cornerman can involve other team members into the play by continued head-hunting. Or the cornerman can screen the original splitter and return down the same side for a jumper *(see Diagram 3-8)*. Diagram 3-8 shows offense from overload pattern of Chapter 7. 3 passes to 5, dips ands screens for 1. Now 3 decides to roll goalward with X1 on his back or 3 comes back over 5 running the blast *(see Chapter 5)*. 3 could stand still and let 5 begin a dribbling screen for 3. 3 could also go screen for 2 to come baseline around 5 while 1 is going to screen for 4.

We like for the cornerman to feed 5 because the forward is usually taller and can make a better overhead pass. If we are facing a zone, we make the pass inside, let 5 go individual; and if the defense sinks, 3 and 1 position themselves for a quick jumper while 2 and 4 hunt the holes on the weakside of the zone.

The cornerman can begin the blast instead of the splitting series by initially dipping toward 1, then breaking around the upper side of 5 *(Diagram 3-8)*. If the blast does not work, 3 can go to the weakside and screen for 2 or 4, putting them, along with 1, into the splitting series.

SECRET REBOUNDING ATTACKS FROM THE CORNER

The weakside cornerman has the best potential to be the greatest rebounder in the game of basketball. By the very nature of his position on the court, he has excellent opportunities provided he is taught the mechanics of this section. Because one of our cornermen was a sophomore on our State Championship team, we used him more as a weakside forward. He responded by grabbing twenty-one plus rebounds per game, most of them offensively. Because of this offensive rebounding, he averaged over eighteen points per game, and he made first team All-State.

All offensive rebounders should watch their defensive player's feet. As the defender picks up one foot, he must pivot to box-out on the other. So the offensive rebounder should step directly toward the foot being picked up. Because the defender has committed himself and because he is somewhat off-balance, it is easy to race by the box-out for the offensive rebound.

Statistics show that most shots, when taken against pressure, carom to the opposite side. So the first decision of the weakside cornerman is can he get around his defender. Should the decision be that he can get around his defender, the rebounder should keep in mind that if it is a man defense, the box-out would have to occur at the top of the key (and most defenders do not blockoff that high); if it is a zone, we do not exchange the weakside. Offensive rebounders must learn not to watch the flight of the ball and not to permit the defender to establish contact.

Should the cornerman decide that he cannot get around the box-out of his defender because his defender is an excellent blockout artist, we send the guard, 2, to screen for 4 *(Diagram 3-8)*. This not only puts the guard where he should be for defensive purposes, but it gives 4 an excellent opportunity to elude his man. However, if 4 sees that he cannot make it to the weakside baseline position prior to the ricochet he will stay high. That maneuver clears out the valuable rebound area for either 3 or 5, who have been fighting boxouts.

Strongside cornermen and post men are taught techniques (we discuss these techniques in Chapter 4 under offensive rebounding for the post men) to get around their box-outs. By virtue of being on the strongside, the side from which the shot is taken, they can better tell if it is too long, too short, or whatever. And we drill them and drill them until they become conscious of making educated guesses as to the length of the shot. The drill that we use is shown in *Diagram 3-10*, and it is augmented by several of our shooting drills, which also involve rebounding.

To help the rebounder decide where the carom will occur, we tell him that medium arc shots or less will rebound longer than higher arc shots. Those shots with good backspin will rebound softer. So the rebounder instantly observes the hardness, the arc height, and the backspin, computes these and races to the spot of the rebound.

Procedure (Diagram 3-10)

1. Line players up in one line as shown.
2. As coach shoots, the first player in line races to the spot where he expects the carom, immediately tips the ball in, then returns to the end of the line.

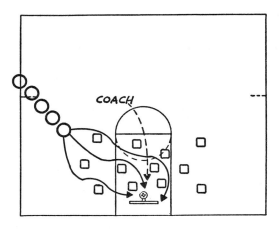

Diagram 3-10

Objectives

1. To teach rebounder to recognize by the height and hardness of the shot where the ball will ricochet.
2. To teach offensive tipping (we teach several and we have a particular time when we want each used).

One thing which aids our offensive rebounding, and we stress offensive rebounding, is that our players are in constant motion. This makes it difficult to box them out. If the rebounder is not boxed out, we want him to catch the ball with both hands, pump fake and go back up strong; or catch the ball with both hands, if he has excellent body control, and while still in the air, lay it back in, using the backboard. If he has been boxed-out and he did not clear the prime rebounding area, we want a high jump, tipping the ball with one hand, keeping it alive for another better positioned rebounder. We only want this tipping process within a few feet of the basket. One hand tipping on the long rebound is wasted; the long rebound should be secured with both hands, giving us a better opportunity to score.

The tip is executed by spreading the fingers and extending them upward, momentarily catching the ball, and flipping it back toward the basket. We use an electric rebounder to teach this spreading and extension.

Offensive rebounders should not be too quick to revert to defense. But if they have made a judgement error in the carom, they should go to the spot where the rebound did come off. Many times, more often than coaches wish to admit, the defensive rebounder will juggle the ball. This presents a golden opportunity for the garbage basket.

We want that second, third, and fourth shot. We don't want to give up too quickly.

SECRETS OF THE BASELINE DRIVE SERIES

This is a series or sequence of moves (a move and its counters) that is unique to the corner position. Because the cornerman receives the initial pass, he has the immediate option of driving the baseline. Hence the baseline drive series permits the cornerman some freedom of action from the inaugural pass, yet keeps him out of the way of inside developments. Several lay-ups and penetrations can occur during any ball game using this series.

The first move is a straight baseline drive. The second maneuver is to drive baseline and shoot a reverse lay-up. The third advance is to drive baseline until cut off, then crossover dribble or reverse dribble to the inside for a hook across the middle. Then we counter this by stopping midway across the middle and shooting the fade away. Stopping midway across the middle, reversing and hooking to the outside is an effective counter to the across the middle moves. This is also an incomparable spot for the twisting jumper.

A counter against being cut off at the baseline is to stop on the outside foot, spread the legs wide, push off inside foot, jump toward the middle area for a jump shot. This move must be practiced to be effective. Most modern players can compensate on the shot for the side movement of the body.

Most teams overplay the cornerman on the baseline side, making it difficult to initiate a drive along the baseline. When this happens, our players drive the middle until cut off, then reverse or crossover dribble to get to the baseline. Across the center cutters delay their cuts until the forward has begun his drive to the baseline.

We also allow the one-on-one maneuvers discussed in Chapter 2, including across the center drives. But we prefer the baseline drive series for two reasons. Usually there is help on the individual driver when coming across the middle; and our offense has two cutters, one following the other in rapid fire fashion, coming across the middle. One of these two is frequently open. So a drive along the baseline, even when stopped, permits penetration and a perfect passing angle, one little drilled against, to the inside cutters coming across the middle.

CHAPTER 4

Developing the Inside Attack
for the Passing-Dribbling Game

As stated before, the fundamental shot in basketball is the long shot because it forces the defense to pressure outside, opening up the middle; and the inside is where games are won or lost, seasons are made or broken. Some coaches believe in attacking inside-out; others prefer outside-in. The passing-dribbling game takes what the defense gives it. If the defense wishes to begin a game by sinking, zone or man, we answer with an outside game. If the defense creates pressure outside, we attack with an inside game. Success comes from the offense dominating these dictates of the defense. Execution, therefore, is paramount. And where Chapter 3 dealt with the execution of the outside game, this chapter unravels the secrets of the inside passing-dribbling attack.

SECRETS OF POSTING

Coaches frequently tell their offensive players: post all mismatches. But how does one post a mismatch? Does the player with greater size simply go to a low post position, and hope that this will enable a teammate to get him the ball. Or are there techniques that will greatly improve the chances?

We have maneuvers that we use to get this mismatched player the ball in the low post, the highest of all percentage scoring areas. This low post cutter does not have to be a forward or a center; he can be a taller guard. And we have found that the posting player can get open more easily when he is cutting from the weakside, the side opposite the ball.

Many free-lance and professional teams constantly try to pre-plan the mismatch. Complete pattern teams incorporate the idea at pre-arranged intervals within their set patterns. And the passing-dribbling game employs posting for all exaggerated mismatches. All coaches need to devise methods of getting smaller defenders on taller attackers. It is an offensive team option which needs to be mastered regardless of system currently used.

Teams can have their center screen for a guard. The guard can cut sharply toward the basket. A switch by the defensive center creates a mismatch for the offensive center. The offensive guard can clearout the low post area, being careful not to cross with the offensive center. Such a cross would result in the defenders' switching back to their original assignments.

Let's first consider this cut coming from the weakside. *Diagram 4-1* shows the center, 5, screening for a guard, 2. As 2 cuts goalward X5 must pick him up or concede the lay-up. 5 immediately rolls toward the bucket, confident that 2 will clear to the corner. 1 will pass to 3 and clear high, keeping his man busy with a weakside exchange. 3 now tries to set up a line of 45 (explained later) with 5. If we can get the ball into 5, his four or five inches will get him an easy jump shot or a power lay-up.

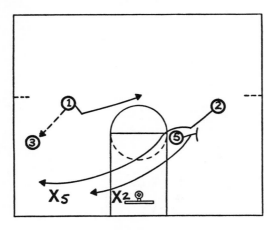

Diagram 4-1

Diagram 4-2 displays a flash pivot cut where 5 has a smaller forward, X3, on him. This mismatched situation occurs frequently, especially when a team is running a pattern similar to Pete Newell's Reverse Action Continuity. Modern man-to-man defenses will not permit 5 a direct route to the ball. So to combat this we use a spin with a reverse pivot maneuver *(Diagram 4-3)*, which enables us to get proper posting position. Now 1 has to maneuver his man into a line of 45. That is our technique whenever the ball is higher than the cutter.

When the ball is lower than the cutter, assuming X3 will not permit 5 a direct route to the ball, we use the maneuver shown in *Diagram 4-3*. It is impossible to spin or reverse pivot and get low post position when the defender

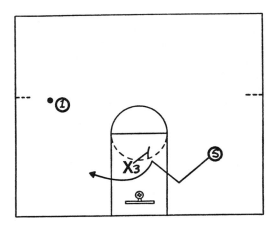

Diagram 4-2

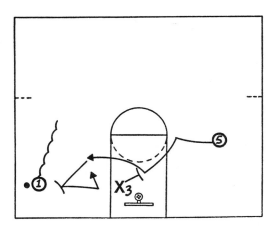

Diagram 4-3

plays lower than the cutter. The cutter would run out of floor space working the maneuver. So we permit 5 to continue high and then go screen for 1, provided 1 does not have a taller defender on him. A simple roll might get the ball inside to 5. If not, it would be up to 1 to establish a line of 45 while 5 uses our technique of jockeying for position.

Diagram 4-4 exhibits the spin and reverse pivot maneuver which we use when the defender plays above the cutter. This maneuver will always get the defender on the cutter's back. A slide toward the baseline with both feet simultaneously will keep the guard on the attacker's back. The footwork begins by allowing the defender to cut the attacker off from his direct route to the ball. The

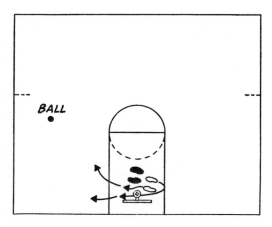

Diagram 4-4

attacker's right foot should split the defender's two feet. He should place his left foot as deeply as possible outside the defender's right foot. The attacker should extend his elbows outward parallel to the floor, and he should pivot on his left foot, making the pivot quickly. As he pivots on his left foot, he swings his right foot completely in front of the defender's body. This puts the defender on the attacker's back. He now quickly slides to low post and maintains this good posting position.

Many of our strongside cuts, designed to get the mismatch, are simple give and go's. We run these whenever the passer is taller than his defender. But our favorite strongside cut comes off a go-behind maneuver *(Chapter 8)*. We call it the buttonhook or the buttonhook with a reverse pivot pinch (see Chapter 2, the section on buttonhooks, for our procedure on this strongside cut).

Weakside players also have an opportunity to post. But there should be only one player, two at most, on the side of the posting if the team is to achieve maximum effectiveness.

Diagram 4-5 relates our overload formation where weakside posting is a possibility *(Chapter 7)*. Let's say a pass has come inside to 5, who immediately pivots to face the basket. Meanwhile, 4 has screened for 1, forcing X1 and X4 to switch, putting the smaller guard, X1, on the taller forward, 4. Now 4 works his weakside posting maneuvers to get X1 on his back.

X1 must play between 4 and the ball or the weakside attacker would have a lay-up by simply moving across the lane. If X1 plays 4 high with denial stance, the defender cannot see the ball. A lob pass from 5 to 4 would get him an easy two foot jumper. But should X1 play below 4, where he could see the man and the ball, the attacker would use the spin and reverse pivot maneuver explained in Chapter 2, except this time the defender would be trying to cut the offensive player high.

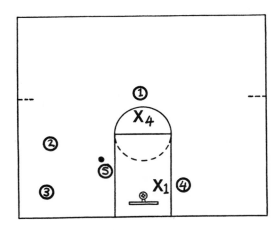

Diagram 4-5

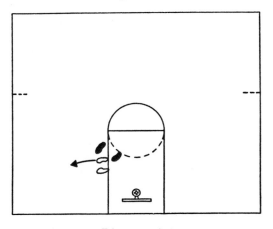

Diagram 4-6

If the weakside or strongside cutting maneuvers do not get our mismatched player open, we leave him at a low post and set up a line of 45. We call this the line of 45 because a line through the passer and the low post man meets the baseline at a 45 degree angle. That is the ideal passing angle because it is the most difficult position for the defender to keep the inside attacker from getting the ball. But we have a maneuver that makes it even easier for the offense.

The defender can cover the stationary low post in only three ways: behind, fronting, or at a side. When the defense plays behind the attacker, it is very easy to toss the ball inside. When the defense plays in front of the low post man, we have a rule which states that the weakside men break to the strongside. Now a lob pass to the far side of the goal results in a lay-up. To aid in receiving this lob pass, the offensive center should bend his inside arm at a 90 degree angle at the elbow. He should have this arm parallel to the floor and just short of contact with the defender. He should extend his baseline arm upward as a signal for the lob pass. His body should be facing the baseline. And he should not go after the lob pass until the ball is directly overhead. Under no circumstances should he straighten the bent elbow. The referee would interpret such a move as pushing. The attacker should merely hold his position, letting the defender make the contact.

Top flight defenders play at the side of the low post with one arm and one hand in front of the attacker. We equalize this defensive coverage with an offensive technique.

Regardless of the side being played, ball side or weakside, we require that our post man place the foot on the side he is being overplayed even with his defenders front foot *(Diagram 4-6)*. This automatically puts the defender on the attackers back. The posting player places his opposite hand in a low position, signifying to the passer to deliver a bounce pass there. The arm on the side of the defender's front foot should be slightly bent at the elbow and extended in the direction of the passer. This arm positioning provides extra leverage to prevent the defender from stealing the bounce pass. A power lay-up usually results.

SECRETS OF HIGH AND LOW POST PLAY

To play a post position, and the inside does not demand any specific physical requirements, a player must be cool under fire. Coolness is a secret to inside excellence, for this attacker will see double and triple teaming tactics during his career. He must diagnose the defense quickly so that he can see or sense if the play developments call for a pass, screen, or shot. Although screening ability is his primary pre-requisite, the inside man's move to pass or shoot must be done with an air of quick confidence.

Receiving the ball in crowded conditions requires a specific stance. The receiver should be crouched, head up, rear down, and back slightly bent forward. The arms should be outstretched, and the feet should be parallel. If possible, the ball should be received as the center executes the jump stop: that gives the inside attacker two pivot feet, making the defensive job more difficult. After receiving the ball, the center should place his elbows out in order to protect the ball to the fullest. It is decision making time, and centers must make that judgement instantly without putting the ball on the floor. Another secret: the center should never take more than one dribble. If more than one dribble is needed, the distance from the bucket is too great to be considered the center position or the fake must have been weak. A quick, smart guard will sink and snake any ball dribbled twice.

Our "Cool Posting Drill" teaches the savvy and stance outlined above.

Cool Posting Drill

Procedure (Diagram 4-7)

1. Rotate from 1 to 2 to 3 to 5 to end of line. The three defenders can be managers, or they can be players who would become part of the rotation.
2. 5 can use any move to get open. 1, 2, and 3 have balls. When 5 does get open, 1, 2, or 3 will pass inside to him. 5 tries to protect the ball from the three defenders by pivoting as long as he can. Later we let 5 drive for a lay-up if he can do it with one dribble.
3. 1, 2, and 3 must constantly re-adjust their positions so that they always have a line of 45. And they must use two handed over the head passing. Passes should not be easily thrown.

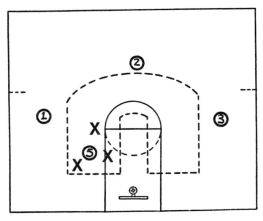

Diagram 4-7

Objectives

1. To teach post man to stay cool even if he is triple teamed.
2. To teach passer to re-adjust to line of 45.
3. To teach one dribble drive.
4. To teach overhead passing.
5. To teach a good receiving stance to the post man.

SECRETS TO MOVING WITHOUT THE BALL

Positioning is the secret to inside play. To get the primary spots on the floor, the center must remain active, constantly moving. That is a purpose of our passing-dribbling substitution rule: anytime movement stops, we bench the immobile player. And that is an advantage of this offensive system: because there is more freedom of movement, players can pick the openings in the defense as they occur. This middle player whether guard, forward, or center must know where the ball is so that he can use the correct movement to get open, and he must know where his teammates are so that he can pass the ball out when faced with a sag.

We do not like for the pivot man to jockey for position. Although it is true that most fouls inside are called on the defense, we feel that jockeying leads to fights and thoughts other than positive basketball. And those thoughts contribute to defeats. Our jockeying, therefore, is restricted to the motion of getting proper position.

In other words, we want all cuts without the ball to be made with a definite purpose in mind. Movement without purpose is wasted motion, and we want to capitalize on every potential scoring opportunity. So we teach several maneuvers to each attacker, keeping those in mind that take advantage of the physical characteristics of our middle men. As the middle man becomes more drilled, more confident, he will begin to use the lines on the court as an aid to his positioning, faking, and shooting.

Fakes that are used inside but originate from the outside have been discussed in other sections: the buttonhooks, for example in Chapter 2. Fakes initiated from inside as well as outside, such as flash pivot cuts, have been or will be developed in other chapters. Any movement across the key can be used by the inside attacker. In fact, almost any outside maneuver can be used inside. However, in this section we will deal only with those fakes peculiar to movement around and inside the key. Where the cut is designed for only one inside spot—side, low, or high—it will be so stated; otherwise any movement discussed here can be used at all inside positions.

Ball side fakes will be considered first. One of the most effective sequence of moves is the sliding spin and the sliding drop-step. They are both taught from the same basic beginning—one used as a counter to the other *(Diagram 4-8)*. The first move is a sliding step from low post to high post. This can be accomplished

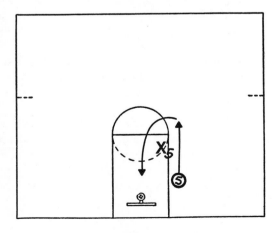

Diagram 4-8

from quick slides to slow slides, depending upon the varying quickness between the attacker and his defender. When 5 reaches a high post and X5 is keeping him from getting the ball, we run either the spin or the drop step, whichever the defense makes available. If the defense has played 5 in a manner by which 5 can drop his right foot between X5 and the ball, we want that done. If, however, we cannot drop step, 5 is to immediately turn to face his defender by dropping his right foot with a front pivot on the goal side of X5 and deeper than X5's body. A quick burst goalward should get 5 open on the goal side for a bounce or lob pass for the lay-up. The defenders coverage provides the key which the attacker can use to determine which move the defense has made available: Nose to nose or behind coverage dictates the drop step; denial defense calls for the spin. The defense must concede either the drop step or the spin. The problem is getting the ball to the attacker at the moment he is open.

The inside V cut is our next progression. This cut is used to go from strongside to strongside as well as from weakside to strongside. If a defensive center drops off his man as the attacker cuts to the weakside, it is easy to V cut behind the defender for good strongside position. In order to accomplish this, the attacker must have a good sense of time: he only has three seconds in the lane. But should three seconds be expiring, the attacker could step out of the lane on the weakside before breaking back to the strongside. In running V cuts we also loop and square.

Looping, in our nomenclature, is moving in one direction, turning a half-circle for one step in the direction from which we came, then completing the turn at least another 180 degrees and heading in the new direction *(Diagram 4-9)*. This gives the center great freedom of movement, and the final decision of direction must be a good one. Without good judgment, a greedy offensive center can clog up the team offense. Looping, as shown in the lower part of Diagram 4-9, can be executed from the weakside.

Squaring is a turn of exactly 90 degrees. An attacker should move hard toward his defender, plant his front foot just short of contact, and front pivot changing directions exactly 90 degrees. *Diagram 4-10* exhibits two examples of a square cut.

Armed with these three cuts and the moves discussed under posting, any attacker should be able to clear himself for a pass. Of course we think the straight cut usually gets the receiver open and an immediate drive to the basket usually gets him the score.

The center races toward his defender, stopping with both feet equal to the defender's *(Diagram 4-11)*, choosing his direction, planting the foot on the side of that direction, swinging the opposite foot completely to the side of his defender. After doing this, the attacker will be facing the baseline if he is going baseline or facing the center court if he is going above his defender. The center's next move will be a long step with his right foot, followed quickly with a short step with the left foot (Diagram 4-11). This puts the defender on the attacker's back with either foot being the pivot foot.

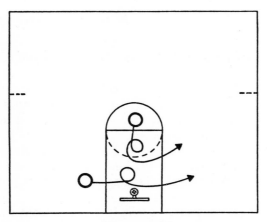

Diagram 4-9

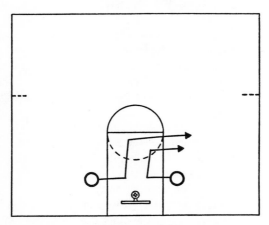

Diagram 4-10

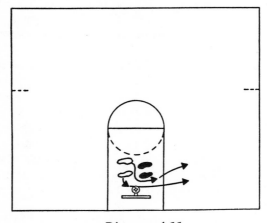

Diagram 4-11

SECRETS TO MOVING WITH THE BASKETBALL

Inside players are first taught the power lay-up. Upon receiving the pass, the attacker should sense or feel the side the defender favors. That side should be the center's pivot foot, and he should swing his other foot using a reverse pivot drop step in front of the defender. He should take a long step and a long dribble, if needed, jump toward the basket, using his inside arm to fend off the defender and lay the ball gently but high on the backboard. This must be practiced going to the right and to the left. On occasions, a fake in an opposite direction of the drop-step might be needed.

Then the player takes that same long drop-step and dribbles for a hook shot. This means that the player must be able to hook left and hook right. He does not have to be a master at the hook shot. But having it in the arsenal will help set up the other maneuvers.

We have a drill that teaches these eight maneuvers (two power lay-ups on the left side of the court, two on right side—two hooks on left side and two on right side). We have the defender follow the attacker across court, and we pass the ball to him as he jumps out of the lane. At the moment the center receives the ball, we have the defender bump him on one side. The attacker immediately drop-steps and drives opposite.

While the above moves are accomplished with the back to the goal, we also like for our attackers to pivot and face the basket. This puts added pressure on the defense because now the jump shot is available.

We teach the inside men the fade away jumper. They are near enough to the basket to easily compensate for jumping away.

Immediately upon turning to the basket, the attacker can drive that direction, or he can crossover and drive the other direction. But only one dribble is permitted on the drive. So the center must make an instant decision and savagely attack the goal. All these moves with the ball that we have discussed in this section are called the center move with counters. It is easy to see how one is a progression from the other, and how each new move is a counter to the defense's stopping the former move.

Inside faking must be held to a minimum. The fake must come only after a move has been defended—a counter, in other words. Why? Because there is little time for maneuvering in this area. Help is only a fraction of a second away.

From the center move, we advance to the power dip. We use this when we receive the ball near the basket so that we will not need a dribble. Upon receiving the ball, without hesitation, the center jumps directly toward the goal, laying the ball in. This must be a quick move such as getting the offensive rebound, landing, and springing back up and toward the goal immediately. If there is contact, the ruling is almost always blocking. Many three point plays result from this move.

Players who receive a pass near the basket or who get an offensive rebound must know how to pump fake. We teach three pump fakes: long, long-short, long-short-short. As the reader can see, each pump fake is a counter for the next. We would not be pump faking unless we had advantageous position. All that remains is the power lay-up. Pump fakes should get the defender into the air or at least off-balance. The long pump fakes should be head high or higher and the short pumps should never go above the chin. Each pump should look like the shot.

INSIDE SECRETS OF SPLITTING THE POST SERIES

How we split the post depends upon the basketball maturity of our center. If he is advanced to a degree where we can expect scoring from him, we permit one-on-one movement immediately after he receives the pass. If he is not a scorer, we immediately split the post and use the center as a screener and a passer.

Our beginning drill is to put all the guards and a center on one end of the court and all the forwards and a center on the other end. We begin with no defense, only cutters; we progress to defensing the cutters; and finally we defense the center. We teach the basic rules before we mix up the teams. In this section we will dwell on the center's responsibility, and we will develop the team movement of our splitting series. We discussed guard and forward play on the splitting series in previous chapters.

The center must remain cool. The perimeter players as well as the center must know our two basic rules: the passer goes first and each cutter must rub shoulders with the center on his cuts. The center must sense or feel where his defender is so that no handoff mistakes will be made. If the center feels defensive pressure on one side, he should hand off to the opposite cutter. If he feels no pressure, he should turn to shoot, for the defensive center is probably sinking and helping on the cutters. Armed with these thoughts, along with the cutter's thoughts *(Chapter 3)*, the center should be capable of making an intelligent decision.

The first two cutters will be the men immediately above and immediately below the center. This can be called off by a cutter going to screen away instead of breaking by the center. In that case, the cutter coming off that screen assumes the splitting responsibilities of the screener. If there is only one cutter near the center, we run the blast *(see Chapter 5)*. Or the passer can call the blast when his first few steps are in the direction of the attacker on the side immediate opposite the passer's side of the center.

In the eight diagrams in this section, we show the pass going into the high post. But we split the post off passes into all inside positions: high, low, or side. Also, recall that it is the responsibility of the cutter to rub his man off on the picker; it is not the responsibility of the center.

Diagram 4-12 is our basic cut. 1 passes into 5 who broke to high post from

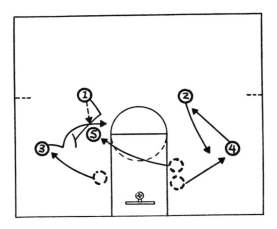

Diagram 4-12

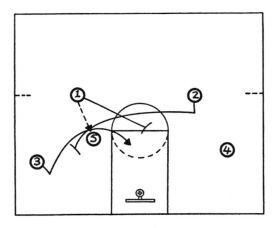

Diagram 4-13

our single stack formation, and 1 dips, setting his man up for the rub-off on 5. 3, who is responsible for timing, dips and cuts off 1's screen. If 3 sees X1 and X3 switching, 3 would fake split and go down 1's side. Or 1 could come back over the center's screen after 3 has cleared by it. All these options are explained in Chapter 3. Notice that the weakside has exchanged, keeping their defenders active and out of the play.

   Diagram 4-13 shows 1 exchanging responsibilities with 2 by passing inside, then screening for 2. This is the key for 2 to assume 1's duties. 2 has dipped to help set up the screen. 2 now becomes the first cutter and 3 is again responsible for timing. If 2 and 4 had exchanged, then 4 would have assumed 1's role in the splitting series.

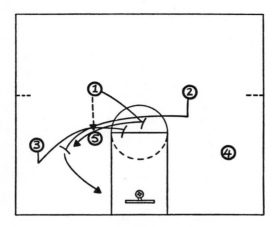

Diagram 4-14

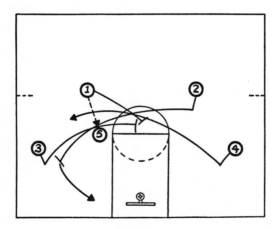

Diagram 4-15

A continuation of this is shown in *Diagram 4-14*. The only difference is 1's counter to X2's weak defensive play, or to X1 and X3 switching on the cuts by 2 and 3. 1 simply cuts back over 3's screen. This gives us good screening activity before the center's pick. The responsibility for proper timing belongs to 1, but his move should occur almost instantly after he had set the screen for 2 if all the cutters are moving at maximum speed.

Diagram 4-15 is the same play, only bringing 4 into the maneuvers. Now 4 is responsible for bringing his cutter off the double screen and around the center's pick. Proper dipping and cutting will always get 4 at least the jumper over 5's screen and at best a lay-up.

Diagram 4-16 is our basic cut again. However, 2 sees his man making a

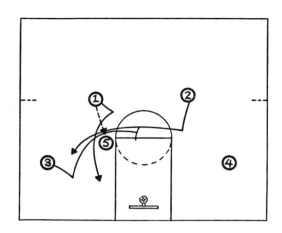

Diagram 4-16

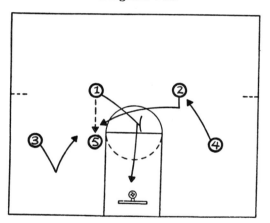

Diagram 4-17

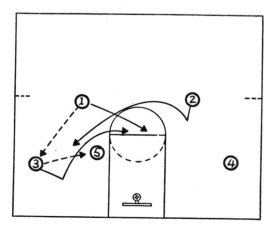

Diagram 4-18

defensive mistake, such as anticipating the weakside exchange, and decides to cut off 5. 1 should have already cleared to the corner, weakside or strongside, according to our rules in Chapter 6. 2 is responsible for proper timing. 2 can use 3's cut for a screen.

Diagram 4-17 displays the screen that was set up in Diagram 4-13. However, X2 tries to fight over the top and X1 switches to cover 2. This defensive mistake followed by 1's roll would put X2 on his back. A backdoor bounce pass would give 1 the lay-up.

Diagram 4-18 shows passing from the corner position. 3 would be the first cutter because he passed inside. 1 can option to run the basic cut, but in this diagram 1 has chosen to help 3 set the double screen for 2 who should easily be open for a driving lay-up. Or if X5 switches, 2 can back out for 5's mismatch on X2.

Diagram 4-19 is a continuation of Diagram 4-18, getting all five men into the play. 1 and 3 have set the double screen for either 2 or 4. In this case, it would be 4 because 2 and 4 are exchanging on the pass inside to 3. 4 comes off of the double screen, and if the defense adjusts, 1 would read it and cut off 3's screen.

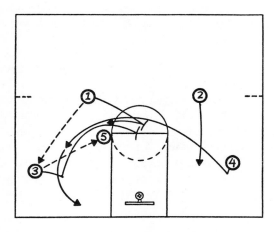

Diagram 4-19

We would rather make the inside pass from the corners or side positions. We show this series from a guard pass to show that splitting the post is extremely effective from any position. We prefer for our guards to pass to the corner and cut to the corner. Then we get the ball inside and begin our splitting series (*see Chapter 7*). There is little to memorize. The players will like it because they make the choices, as is true throughout the passing-dribbling game. There can always be at least one more screen by permitting the weakside men to screen for each other on all passes.

Splitting the post is difficult, if not impossible, to defend. There is too much screening for a man defense to cover without a little confusion. And that confusion should result in an easy shot. We drill constantly on this maneuver. We allow the players to initiate imaginative moves off of it.

SECRETS TO FREEING ONESELF INSIDE

Many center moves versus denial defense were discussed in the sections on secrets of posting and secrets to moving without the basketball. After mastering those two sections, any center should be able to free himself. It is important that he stay on the move. Any lack of movement aids the defense. It is equally important that he make sharp, angled cuts, executing them quickly with as much body control as possible.

However, we teach two distinct techniques just for defeating denial defense when our regular cuts are not creating the openings. First, we break the center high, having him line up at weakside low post, dipping completely to the basket, before breaking. Proper denial defense cannot watch both the man and the ball as this break occurs. The moment the defender turns to watch the ball, we back off from hand contact and break to the hole. If the defender should watch the cutter at the expense of losing sight of the ball, we run the dummy lob pass play for an easy lay-up.

But if this maneuver fails, we line up in a point guard with two wing men. As the center dips to the basket the strongside wing man reverses the ball to the point guard to what was the weakside guard. The center reverse pivots, putting his denial defender on his back. Now the post man has a line of 45 with the original weakside wing man.

Although denial man defense is the best or denial inside while in a zone is adequate, if our players continue moving at sharp angles, it is only a matter of time until we can penetrate the interior. And if our little men have been developed as in Chapter 3, the job of getting the ball inside is that much easier.

SECRETS OF SETTING UP
THE INSIDE BACKDOOR OPTION

Centers, unlike guards, have their backs to the basket as a cutter is going backdoor. So centers must sense the cut coming. They must bend at the knees and flip the bounce pass back-handed, using both hands. The pass must have sufficient lowness to get beneath the center's defender's hands and beneath the cutter's defender's hand. But it must, at the same time, have sufficient depth to bounce at least to the cutter's waist.

We have a drill which helps to teach this passing technique to our centers. It is also an option within our passing-dribbling game's splitting the post series. We call it the center's backdoor drill.

Procedure (Diagram 2-4)

1. Line squad up behind 1. Rotate from 1 to 2 to 3 to end of line 1.
2. 3 dips completely to the basket, then breaks high, stopping in a jump stop just above the foul line.
3. 2 dips and cuts backdoor. 1 dips and splits around the center. 3 may hit either with a side bounce pass, like passing to a backdoor cutter. Or 3 could keep the ball and go one-on-one.
4. After the passing becomes adequate, we add a defender on all three and let them split the post, backdoor, go one-on-one or whatever decision that must be made to counteract the defense. If it was a bad decision, we stop and explain why.

Objectives

1. To teach the backdoor cut.
2. To teach the backdoor pass.
3. To teach splitting the post.
4. To help teach savvy, that ingredient of all championship teams.

If the center is the backdoor cutter, he must learn to keep his eyes on the ball until it settles in his hands. Too many centers fight receiving passes. They must learn to give with the ball.

We do not use a drill to teach the center a backdoor cut. We did, however, have individual cuts that utilized the backdoor cut (see section on movement without the ball).

SECRETS OF SETTING UP THE LOB PASS OPTION

There are three times when we set up the lob pass, and the centers must recognize them instantly. The perimeter men must be able to deliver the pass, discussed in the last chapter; therefore, they, too, must recognize the situation developing. We have no other keys that call it.

Anytime a low post man is fronted, we have a rule that calls for the weakside to be cleared out *(see Chapter 6)*. This leaves no defenders on the weakside to either draw the charge or steal the lob pass, and the low post is being fronted. A lob pass to the low post on the far side of the basket would result in a lay-up.

Low post men must learn the technique that was discussed in the section on secrets of posting. When they use this technique, they are assured of receiving the lob pass near the basket.

The second situation where the perimeter and center cooperates concerns the flash pivot cut. This time, however, we give a key. Most modern day defenses, zone or man, will not permit the cutter a direct route to the basketball. When the defender cuts off the flash pivot, he often has his back to the ball. If the offense has split the defender, we expect the spin with reverse pivot move that was discussed earlier. If the attacker is even with the defender, we give the key, raising of the head, to the guard to lob the pass goalward. The defender cannot see the lob coming: he has his back to the ball defending the flash pivot cut. The inside attacker plants his outside foot, pushing off it hard and takes a one step leap toward the basket, catching the ball and laying it in in one motion. This option works equally well against both a zone and a man defense. It is run anytime the defender stops a flash pivot's cut by turning his back to the ball. But if the defender cuts the flash pivot's direct route off by facing the ball, the attacker should not permit the defender any body contact. Because the defender has no contact with the cutter, it would be impossible to prevent a quick slashing cut (Diagram 4-6) to the strongside for good posting position. So getting by the flash pivot defender into a strongside low post position or running the lob pass option serve as counters to each other.

The third situation is usually found against zones. It occurs whenever the attacker gets between his man and the goal. The center must be adept at using the reverse pivot or front pivot so that he can maintain this advantageous inside position. It is like gaining inside offensive rebounding position *(Diagram 4-20)*. The inside attacker catches the lob pass and lays it in all in one motion. Diagram 4-20 shows such a lob pass from our overload *(Chapter 7)* formation against a 2-3 zone. This situation can be run against a man defense. Its key, which must be recognized by the passer, is not any obvious signal: it is called by the cutter cutting behind his defender.

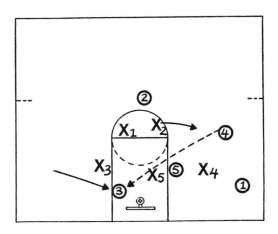

Diagram 4-20

SECRETS OF THE LINE OF 45 OPTION

The center's responsibilities in setting up the line of 45 are two fold. He must recognize the defensive coverage on him: for example, is he covered at the side, in the front, or behind. His second duty is to counter that defensive coverage. When faced with fronting, we clear the weakside. When faced with behind tactics, the center bends forward at the waist, but keeps his weight backward. The center holds his arms straight toward the passer. As the pass is delivered we want the center to jump stop toward the pass, but we want this forward movement to be ever so slight. This gives the center two pivot feet, better for faking, and keeps him closer to the basket. We discussed the center's responsibility when faced with side coverage in the section on posting. When executing his techniques properly, the center would have the ball and a drop step toward the basket on his defender. One dribble, at most—we never allow the center more than one, should give him the power lay-up.

SECRET INSIDE REBOUNDING ATTACKS

We hit the offensive boards hard. Every shot taken in practice is followed by the word *"Boards."* This indicates that we anticipate its being missed and that we want three men after the ricochet.

First, we must decide where it will carom. We quickly compute three things: how far from the basket was the shot taken; how high was the arc; and what was the angle in relation to the backboard. The farther the shot the longer the rebound will be. The shorter the arc the longer the rebound will be. And the ball usually caroms off the board at the same angle which it hits it only to the opposite side.

To help us decide on these things, we check two items before every away game. We want to know how tight the rims are. If the rims are loose, the ball will rebound shorter. We also want to know the brand name of the game ball. Wilson Jets rebound higher and longer than the Spaulding 100.

We have already discussed our strongside rebounding plans from the backcourt and corner positions. Our center is nearer the basket, and we try to get him inside rebounding position by using the secret little techniques that are natural to all great rebounders. Of course, if he is unable to get inside position, he is to use the same tipping ideas as the cornermen *(see Chapter 3)*.

We have an original tipping drill that has made our rebounders sensational. We fill a volleyball with so much air that it will almost burst. This makes it lighter and more active, harder to tip into the basket. And we play a game to ten baskets. A player must win by at least two baskets. Here are the rules of the game:

    1. Player A tosses the ball over the rim against the board toward Player B. It
       can be tossed with as much spin and as much force as A likes as long as the

ball will carom into the free throw lane. After a score, Player B tosses the ball on the board for Player A's free tip.

2. All tipping must be done from a jump and with only one hand. Player B gets the first free tip. After Player B tips ball against the board, either A or B can tip. No person can tip twice in succession unless the ball has hit the board or the rim.

It does not take long for the players to realize that a tip off the board, very softly, will go in better than the tip to the rim. The players quickly realize the value of inside position. The ball will not go in many times even though it is tipped softly; consequently, the players realize the importance of the second, third, and fourth efforts. The game is fun, and the players can play it on outdoor courts in the heat of the summer. There they are working on rebounding position, tipping, second and third efforts, in sweltering heat and enjoying it.

We make use of two techniques to secure inside rebounding position when faced with a blockout. The first technique has the same footwork as our spin and reverse pivot move that gets us by the defender who has cut us off on the flash pivot move. We place one foot between the widely spaced feet of the defensive rebounder. We have our upper arms parallel to the floor, and our lower arms and hands vertical to the floor, pointing upward. This not only gives us a leverage to pry around box-outs but it has our arms in proper rebounding position for the quick carom. And there is no danger of a pushing foul. The pivot is made on the foot opposite the one that was between the feet of the defender. The reverse pivot spin is better than the front pivot because it enables us to lose contact with the defender, causing him to either guess where we are or take his eyes off the rebound to find us. Now we have our back to the basket, but a 180 degree spin puts us facing it. And we are at least parallel to the defender. We then go after the ball, like in our volleyball rebounding game.

If we find the defender executing his blockout too quickly, we will make use of our second technique. We will make contact with the defender on one side and also give him a little dip fake in that direction, but we will keep our balance underneath the other foot. As soon as the defender begins to move in the direction where he feels our contact, we front pivot in the other direction. We are now at least even with the defender and possibly even in front of him.

When facing a zone defense, it is much easier to get inside rebound position. Most of the time, when the ball is shot, the cutters are already in inside position. We like to spread the zone, then penetrate it. This eliminates their triangle, leaving at least one primary rebounding area open. Most zone defenders watch the flight of the ball, making it easy to get around them.

To sum up, the offensive rebounder should always be in motion , a requirement in the passing-dribbling game. He should never watch the flight of the ball, concentrating instead on securing good foot position. He should tabulate where he thinks the carom will be and aggressively go get the ball. He should never give up on the rebound until it has been firmly secured by the defender.

CHAPTER 5

Developing the Two and Three Men
Options of the Passing-Dribbling Game

Individual techniques, presented in the first four chapters, are the backbone of the first fundamental rule of the passing-dribbling game. Those techniques must become habitual, a state which only years of drilling produce. That drilling, which eliminates missed individual scoring opportunities, takes place on the playgrounds, on the streets, where two or three gather to play basketball.

But individual techniques are not all there is to the passing-dribbling game. The passing-dribbling game is team basketball at its best. Two and three men games are apparent in all team offenses. And that is what this chapter intends to develop. The next chapter will codify those one, two, and three men mechanics into a smooth, workable, organized team pattern.

SECRETS TO BREAKING DOWN THE
PASSING-DRIBBLING GAME OFFENSE

The passing-dribbling game is broken into a two and a three men game. The two men game is separated further into individual cuts and into screens and picks. The three men game is reduced to action involving the ball and to action away from the ball.

The passing-dribbling offense is really three games condensed into one. There is the screening game which is part of both the passing and the dribbling offense. There is the cutting game which is only a passing offense. And there is the driving game which is part of the dribbling offense. All games deteriorate and victimize all defenses. But the screening and driving games work best against man defenses, and the passing game destroys the zones.

EIGHT METHODS OF BEGINNING THE OFFENSE

Before developing the two and three men games further, players must learn the eight cutting options off of the basic rule: strongside guard cuts through while the weakside exchanges. Although strongside guards acquire these eight different ways to initiate the passing-dribbling offense, they realize that they may contrive many others. These options, along with those already discussed, make it difficult for denial pressure to force the offense out of its attack.

When used sparingly, these eight maneuvers give the offense a new look. Often one of the basic eight is required to commence the pattern against denial defenses. When the techniques discussed earlier do not free the cornermen for a penetrating pass, players open the passing-dribbling game with these counters.

Counter one exhibits a guard and a cornerman interchanging, permitting the offense to take advantage of skills of certain attackers versus certain defenders *(Diagram 5-1)*: for example, if 1's man is not a good denial defender, 1 and 3 exchange without a screen, making it easier to get the penetrating pass into 1. This exchange is also an excellent maneuver when 3 is tall and X1 is small. A screen down by 3 for 1, assuming 3 started the offense at a guard, would get 3 at a low post with X1 on him, creating a perfect mismatch. At the least, this offers another entry into the attack.

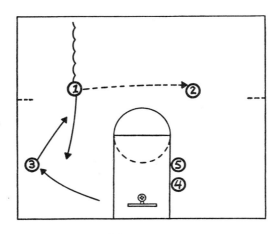

Diagram 5-1

Counter two *(Diagram 5-2)* displays 1 dribbling into front court, waiting for 3 to free himself. Should 3 be unable to get open, 1 could pass to 2 and break through to the new strongside. We are now in the overload formation *(Chapter 7)* ready to attack a zone or a man. The double screen on the baseline, set by 4 and 5, offers an opportunity to get 1 a jumper. But 1 must cut off 4's shoulder to lose

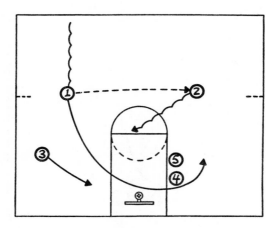

Diagram 5-2

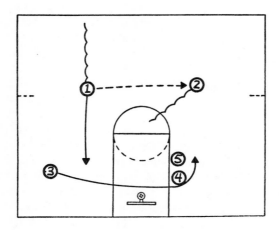

Diagram 5-3

his man. 2 can dribble to the point position to attack from the weakside or reverse the action for a strongside option.

1 has again dribbled down the floor and 3 is again unable to get open *(Diagram 5-3)*. 1 goes to exchange with 3, but 3 has cleared out to the opposite side. The same options that were open to 1 in the last counter is now open to 3. 2 again dribbles to the point, and the offense is ready to attack strongside or weakside with its many options.

Diagram 5-4 exposes a perfect mechanism versus pressure or denial defense. As 1 dribbles ball into front court, he can choose between a pass to 2 and go screen or a dribbling screen with 2. This diagram shows the pass and screen.

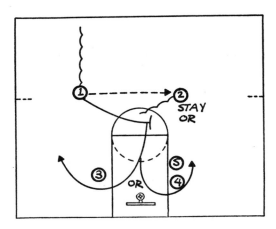

Diagram 5-4

Not only does this give an entry into the patterned offense, but it gives our guards extra scoring opportunities: 2 has the area around the free-throw circle cleared for one-on-one maneuvers; and 1 has screens on both sides of the lane, a double-screen on left side by 4 and 5 and a single screen on the right side by 3.

From this positioning it is easy to get into the passing game with the overload formation or into the dribbling game with the weaves. 1 could break high on the wing, permitting the forward, 3 or 4, to break to the corner. 5 could break to the ball side, giving the offense its overload formation. Or 1 could break to the corner with 3 or 4 taking the wing, putting the offense into the overload. Both maneuvers defeat denial pressure, the toughest of all defenses.

When a team has a good inside man and an exceptional forward, as we possessed one year, *Diagram 5-5* provides an impeccable beginning for the passing game. 1 makes the penetrating pass into 3. 1 cuts weakside high to prevent any possible double-teaming by X1 and X5 on 5. 5 now uses the moves described in the last chapter to get open breaking across the lane. 3 and 5 work the two men games, especially the blast, described later in this chapter. Reversing the ball would get 1 a good shot against zones.

Diagram 5-6 illustrates an option that a team should use when it has a talented guard and a good center. 1 passes inside to 3 and goes to screen the opposite guard. Many successful counters can occur with this maneuver. If 2 is taller than X1, and if X1 switches on 2, 2 could post low. If 1 is taller than X2, 1 would roll and post low as 2 breaks high for the jump shot. But if the attackers and defenders were equal in size, we would have the guard continue to the corner. 5, being the second cutter under our rules, would try to establish post position. Now we could run the splitting series, reverse the ball, have any two men game operating, or overload to attack all zones.

Or 1 could crossover dribble, reverse, or in some way change his direction

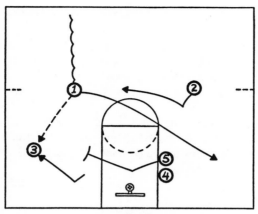

Diagram 5-5

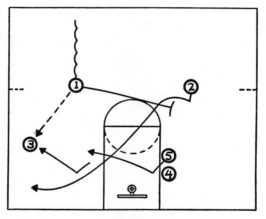

Diagram 5-6

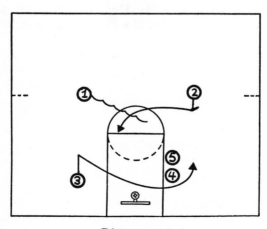

Diagram 5-7

and drive into the top half of the circle to set a pick for 2 *(Diagram 5-7)*. 2 dips to set his man up for the pick. Upon seeing this, 3 would clearout the side, running his man into the double-screen set by 4 and 5. 1 can hit 2, who has half of the court to work his one-on-one magic; or 1 could hit 3, who has come off a double-screen, for a jump shot.

Diagram 5-8 is a continuation from the last example. In this case, 1 does not stop his dribble, but 2 and 3 continue their cuts. 1, therefore, has begun the dribbling game (see sections on weaves and Chapter 8).

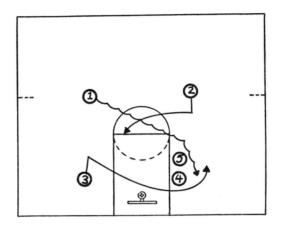

Diagram 5-8

The dribbling game can start from the last two options, and denial defense cannot stop either part play. Both options keep the ball in the center of the court, the best place for offenses to begin. These eight methods of completing the penetrating pass has made the initial phase of the passing-dribbling game almost unstoppable.

Basketball, to us, is a science, a chess-like game. And its moves are all made, offensively and defensively, in the region of two or three attackers and defenders. Five men basketball is only an outgrowth of continuous two and three men games.

THE TWO MEN GAME

A. The Cuts

Offenses, to be effective, must have pre-arranged two-men plays that are drilled on until perfected. The passing-dribbling offense is no exception. While the two men involved in the two men game are cooperating to take instant advantage of a defensive weakness, the other three teammates are keeping their defenders busy, and they are setting up the next part option in case the two men play does not work.

Cutting is one of the three primary ways of executing an offense against both the zone and the man. Socrates said students learn by doing. Players should, therefore, drill until the cuts become second nature. And coaches should tell their players the when, the why, and the how of cutting.

Players learn individual cuts first, utilizing two attackers, a passer and a receiver, and two defenders in drill fashion. The reader may think that his players will learn their cuts by just talking about them, but this is not true.

1. The Give and Go. The give and go is merely a pass followed by the passer's cutting between the receiver and the passer's defender. A return pass usually results in a driving lay-up. The receiver should lead the cutter, passing to the spot best shielded from the defender. This spot differs with each cut.

If the defender does not move in the direction of the pass and does not keep his eyes on his man, a defensive mistake will have been made which can be exploited by the give and go. If the defender does move in the direction of the pass, the backdoor is the counter. A live two-on-two half court drill educates players to these options.

2. The Backdoor. When a defender plays between a cutter and the ball, the cutter should take one step toward the ball. If there is no reaction or if there is yet another step taken toward the ball by the defender, the cutter pushes off his outside foot and breaks hard behind the defender. It is the counter cut to the give and go.

Both the backdoor and the give and go work against the zones. The backdoor works best against the zone when executed a distance from the ball, such as when the ball is out front and the backdoor occurs behind the back line of the zone for the lob pass option.

3. The Middle Cut. This is our primary cut against zones, sagging man-to-mans, and combination type defenses. Against the pressure defenses, the passer cuts first; against the sags, the middle cut occurs first.

When a defensive man who is not directly involved with the ball, a weak-side defender for example, makes a defensive mistake, such as facing the ball or taking his eyes off his man, this attacker middle cuts, breaking between his defender and the ball. By the time the defensive man recovers, the penetrating pass, possibly even the shot, should have eroded the effectiveness of the defense on that one possession. The middle cut, therefore, is a cut by an attacker off the ball, and his cut is the same as in the give and go. Its best use is against the zone whose defender repeatedly makes the mistake of not knowing where both the man and the ball are.

4. The Go Behind. In our nomenclature, this is a pass and follow, going behind the receiver for a return pass, utilizing the receiver as a screen. To set it up, the original passer must dip and change directions so that his man will not fight over the top, making the return pass impossible.

We use the go behind and its kindred, the blast, so often that we named one of our basic team patterns after it. The go behind is used mainly to set up the next option; the blast is used primarily for scoring. The go behind is merely a cut; the blast offers twelve different scoring options.

Players must never use the go behind when teams are double-teaming the ball. The go behind should be used when the forward has a height advantage on his defender or when the center is an excellent screener and good inside scorer. These techniques and theories are discussed thoroughly in Chapter 8.

5. *The Flash Pivot.* Constant cutting through the post area is a trademark of the passing-dribbling game, whether faced with zone or man coverage. And the most used cut is the flash pivot.

To flash pivot, a weakside forward or a center breaks from the weakside, cutting across the lane sharply, after having taken a dip. The technical aspects of getting open have been discussed in Secrets of Posting in Chapter 4.

The flash pivot keeps continuity flowing inside. It keeps pressure on the inside defenders, where a simple mistake would give the offense a high percentage shot. And even though the opposition plays excellent defense, we have techniques to tilt the situation in favor of the offense.

6. *The Buttonhooks.* This is the flash pivot coming from the strongside. Its mechanics have also been discussed in the section on posting (Chapter 4).

Anytime the go behind is run, the buttonhook is run. Should a pass not come inside on the ensuing posting maneuver, the buttonhooker would clearout to the weakside, leaving the strongside low post area cleared for the next cutter.

B. The Screens and Picks

Cuts are not the only primary means of scoring from a two men play. Screening offers another. Screens on the ball, in our vernacular, are considered two men plays; screens away from the ball are three men plays. Those part plays are part of the passing-dribbling game, and when executed properly, they are virtually unstoppable. As we develop the patterns *(Chapters 7, 8, and 9)* we will discuss each part play in its proper sequence. All two men plays are taught with a two on two drill until execution is perfected.

1. *Screen and Roll.* All teams screen and follow up the defensive switch with a roll. When executed properly, a shot should result. If the defense switches early, the roll would put the dribbler's defender on the roller's back. An inside pass gives the roller a high percentage shot. If the defense switches late, the dribbler should have the jump shot. When a big man screens and a small man dribbles, the screen and roll is extremely effective.

We sprinkle this part play throughout our offense, constantly trying to create the mismatch. Should the defense make even the slightest mistake, we should net two points. Should there be improper execution or distinguished defensive play, the only thing wasted is time.

The screen and roll is not run when the defense double-teams any crossing of the ball. And it should not be run, except in rare cases, against the zones.

2. The Blind Pick. When setting the blind pick, the picker must allow the defense one complete step before contact or it is an offensive foul. The blind pick can be set two ways: facing the defender who is to be picked or turning his back on the defender. The passing-dribbling game uses both methods.

It is the responsibility of the cutter to run his defender into the screen. To accomplish this, the cutter must start in one direction, change the direction, and rub shoulders with the screener as he cuts by.

When the cutter is setting up his defender, he should observe the side his defender is playing. If it is ball side, the cutter should run his man over the outside shoulder of the picker. If it is the side away from the ball, the cutter should dip his man into the inside shoulder of the screener.

This blind pick maneuver works well on the ball (blind pick) and away from the ball (rub-off). The passing-dribbling game makes use of both. When used on the ball, it is usually a point man having a pick set by a center. If we are in 14 or 13, we would swing the wing on that side, setting up a drive for the guard all the way to the goal (see Chapters 7, 8, and 9). The blind pick by a forward for a guard on a backdoor cut offers a golden opportunity for the center to unload a pass to that guard for a lay-up. All the options involving the blind pick, and they are plentiful, will be shown in Chapters 7, 8, and 9. The rub-offs, picks away from the ball, are discussed in a later section in this chapter.

Offensively the counter is for the picker to immediately cut to the ball. If there is no switch, assuming the cutters run a good cut, a lay-up will result. If there is a switch, the screener is open.

3. The Inside Screen. In our vernacular, the inside screen is a pass and the passer goes to screen for the receiver. Depending upon the defensive adjustments, the offense can select several options. A screen and roll, for example, would be an excellent counter to the early switch. A late switch would get the receiver a driving lay-up, as would fighting over the top. A slide through by the defender on the receiver would get the receiver the jump shot.

As simple as this maneuver is, we encourage its use between the passing guard and the receiving forward at the inception of the passing-dribbling game. Many of our patterns display this (Chapters 7, 8, and 9).

When faced with a double-teaming defense, this option, like all involving the ball and two attackers, should not be run. It is far better for the offensive team to use the action away from the ball.

4. The Dribbling Screen. When the ball handler dribbles toward a teammate, that teammate must clear the area or set his man up for the screen by the dribbler. If the area is cleared, the attacker has fewer than five seconds to dribble. If the dribbling screen is to occur, we are in the weave (see Chapter 1). All the options that occurred in the three on three drill discussed in Chapter 1 can occur. And the offense should recognize them instantly and take advantage of them. Correct decisions lead to checkmate.

The passing-dribbling game has many ways of getting into the dribbling screen. But it is used only when employing the dribbling game; therefore, it is not used against a zone defense.

5. The Screen and Go Behind. Diagram 5-9 illustrates the screen and go behind maneuver. 1 passes to 3 and goes to screen for 3. 3 drives around 1's screen, putting into operation all the options of the inside screen maneuver. Usually X1 will fight to get position back on 1, forgetting that 1 can still be a strongside player. This mental oversight occurs because X1 sees 3 dribbling away from 1. When X1 does make this defensive mistake or when the man whom 3 is dribbling toward clears out his side, 1 should dip and change directions, running his defender into 3's pick. Now the many options of the blind pick apply.

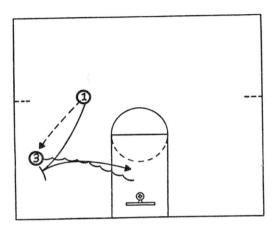

Diagram 5-9

The passing-dribbling game makes use of this maneuver sporadically. Usually it nets two points, but frequent use would curb its effectiveness.

6. Secrets of the Explosive Blast. The blast is a two men play that coaches have not developed to its fullest potential. Free-styled or patterned offensive systems can make use of this two men play provided they leave no more than those two attackers on one side of the front court. Any combination of guard to forward, guard to center, or forward to center can run the blast productively. It is most effective when a small man cooperates with a big man.

The pivot by the inside receiver keys the success of the blast. This inside attacker should receive the ball as close to the lane as possible. A change of direction, the dip for example, will get him close *(Diagram 5-10)*. When 5 receives the ball, he can use either the jump stop or the stride stop, provided he can use his inside foot as his pivot foot.

As 1 begins his cut, 5 is facing him. 1 aims his cut as though he is going to run over 5. Just before contact, 5 reverse pivots on his right foot, placing his back

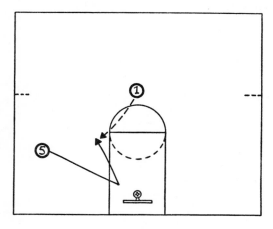

Diagram 5-10

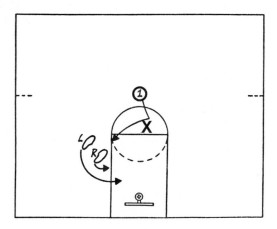

Diagram 5-11

to 1 and X1 *(Diagram 5-11)*. 1 rubs his left shoulder with 5's right shoulder as he cuts by.

Now is decision making time, the moment of truth. Successful part plays have counters for any defensive tactic or adjustments. And the offense must permit the defense to dictate the option that is to be used.

To determine that option, 5 watches X5. But should 5 make a mistake and misread X5, the blast has built in counters to counteract the mistake.

Diagram 5-12 exhibits the hand-off drive. We run the hand-off drive when 5 has successfully picked X1 and X5 does not switch to 1. The hand-off pass to 1 leaves him open for a driving lay-up.

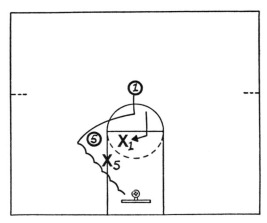

Diagram 5-12

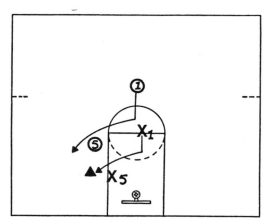

Diagram 5-13

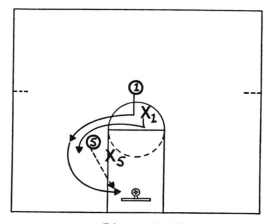

Diagram 5-14

But if 5 fails to pick X1, then we run the jumper by the big man *(Diagram 5-13)* or the delayed pass *(Diagram 5-14)*. X1 calls this option by his coverage. If X1 tries to slide through between 5 and X5, 5 would shoot his jump shot over the smaller defender, X1.

If X1 tries to fight over the top, X5 would stay with 5. That would cue 1 to break hard toward the basket for a delayed pass from 5 and a lay-up. X1 would definitely be behind 1 if he goes over the top and 1 has run a half-decent cut.

Diagram 5-15 displays the screen and roll. When X1 and X5 switch on the hand-off, we run the screen and roll. Even a perfect switch would give us an advantage. X5, the defensive center, would have to cover 1, the small guard, giving us an advantage in outside maneuverability. While 1 is dribbling back outside, 5 would be posting X1 low, giving us an advantage in size inside. A pass into 5, who is bigger than X1, would result in an easy five feet jumper or a power lay-up.

Diagram 5-16 exposes the blast. Remember that 5 is pivoting on his inside foot, right foot, and putting X1 on his back. Now if X5 switches too quickly onto 1, 5 takes a long one bounce dribble for a lay-up. To legally accomplish this, the ball must be out of 5's hand before he picks up his right foot. And 5 should take a long step with his left foot, keeping X1 on his back while picking up the one bounce for a lay-up. If X5 delays for a fraction of a second, 1 has the driving lay-up.

Diagram 5-17 shows X1 and X5 both sinking behind 5 for the switch. A hand-off to 1 gives him the jump shot. Or 1 can dribble to his right and we run the screen and roll or get the mismatch low. We also give 1 the jumper over the screen when X1 goes behind X5 on his defensive coverage.

Diagram 5-18 discloses the final phase of the blast. Let's say that the defense has been perfect and 5 has made a mistake, because even perfect defense cannot stop the blast. Should this happen, 5 begins a dribbling screen for 1. And it would be a screen down, the most difficult of all screens to defend. 1 has the jump shot over 5's screen; or 1 can move back outside, setting up another part play. Or if X5 switches to 1 and X1 picks up 5, we would have the same situation described in Diagram 5-15.

7. *The Screen Down with a Roll*. This is the second most difficult screening maneuver to defend. For some reason, cutters breaking away from the goal give defenders a false sense of security. The passing-dribbling game uses the screen down with the ball and a dribbling screen as described at the end of the section on the blast and the screen down with a roll when the ball is not involved.

When the ball is involved, it is a dribbling screen, as 5 dribbling down to screen for 1. Not only does 1 have the jumper, but if there is a switch, 5 would have a small guard on him and 5 could post for the high percentage shot.

Powell Valley's first trip to the state tournament was possible to a large degree because of the three play: a screen down and a roll away from the ball *(Diagram 5-19)*. It has netted us many jump shots and lay-ups. Let's say 1 has passed to 3 and is cutting away from the ball. 5 has screened down for 4. 5

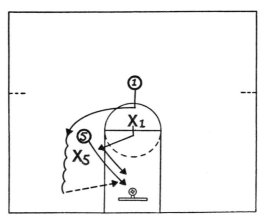

Diagram 5-15

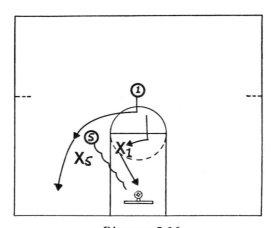

Diagram 5-16

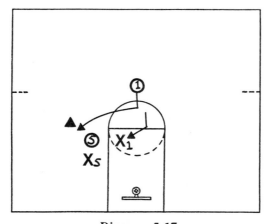

Diagram 5-17

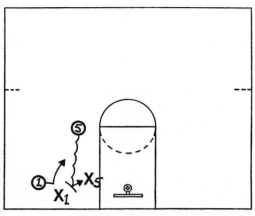

Diagram 5-18

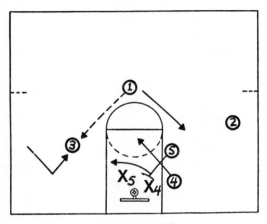

Diagram 5-19

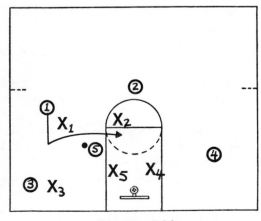

Diagram 5-20

screens the outside shoulder of 4 and rolls immediately, putting X4 on his back. If X4 chooses to go with 4, he will be too late to prevent the jump shot. If X5 switches to 4, 5 will get the lay-up.

When running this option with a big man screening for a small man, there is no way the defense can adjust. The three play can start with 1 possessing the ball.

THE THREE MEN GAME

When the defense double-teams a gathering of the ball and two attackers, we run the blast, the cutting game, or our three men game. These (two men and three men) games are really misnamed because all five men are involved in the action. Plays are keyed and continuity kept by the rules outlined in Chapter 6. The chess game is won or lost where these events take place.

We break the three men game into action involving the ball and action away from the ball. The action involving the ball can be run against man defenses while the action away from the ball can be run against all defenses.

A. Action Involving the Ball

Splitting the post and fake splitting the post, unfolded in the last chapter, comprises the passing-dribbling game's three men maneuvers involving the ball. Both have been fully covered.

But players can confuse the calling of the blast (two men play) with the calling of the splits (a three men play). Both begin with a pass inside and a dip off the receiver. The key is the initial step prior to the dip. The blasting-splitting drill not only acquaints the players with the call, but it helps develop both the blast and the splits.

The Blasting-Splitting Drill

Procedure (Diagram 5-20)

1. Line players up five on five in the overload formation. Let 1 pass the ball inside to 5.
2. 1 gets the first cut. If 1's initial step is away from 3, it is the split. If 1 dips toward 3, as shown, it is the blast. 2 and 4 should be exchanging or clearing.
3. 2 can be added into the action. Should 1 call the blast 2 and 3 can begin the splits. Or 3 can backdoor while 2 and 5 blast. Or 1 and 2 can split. Many combinations are evident.

Objectives

1. To teach players to recognize which call 1 makes.

2. To teach the blast and the splits.
3. To teach defense of the blast and the splits.

B. Action Away from the Ball

Two weakside men cooperating with a ball handler illustrates a three men play away from the ball. The ball handler's and a screener's working on the strongside while two men try to gain an advantage on the weakside demonstrates a four men play. And if the other attacker is trying to set up an individual cut or maneuvering to keep floor balance, we have five men in the offensive maneuver.

Diagram 5-19 is a good example of a four men play. Suppose 1, instead of cutting away from the pass, runs the blast with 3. While 5 and 4 are setting up the screen down and roll. Now if 2 has read this and is trying to set his man up for a baseline cut or is breaking outside for an outlet pass, we would have a five men play. So let's develop the basic three men plays of the passing-dribbling game.

1. The Offside Screen. The offside screen is a positive screen set just short of contact by one member on the weakside for a teammate on that same side. Its sole purpose is to get the cutter open. The cutter has no responsibility other than cutting by the shoulder of the screener. The screener has the responsibility of coming up to but not against the defender he is screening. Once he has set the screen he should reverse pivot and roll toward the goal. If the screener sets the screen with the lower half of his body, the screener's man must switch. The roll back toward the basket would put the cutter's defender on the screener's back.

The passing-dribbling game uses this screen to get the cutter a step on his defender for a quick pass and a jump shot or on the reverse pivot a lay up for the screener. It can force switches and set the screener up after a few passes for the mismatch. If for no other reason than forcing the defense to constantly switch men, thereby confusing it, the offside screen is worth teaching.

2. The Pass and Screen Away. On the offside screen, the screener does not have to touch the ball to set several such screens during any possession. On the pass and screen away, the screener first passes the ball and immediately goes to screen for a teammate on the weakside. We have found that the defenders are more conscious of the offside screen when it is preceded by a pass. The pass and screen away is usually reserved for a guard, while the offside screen is used by a center or a forward.

The pass and screen away's primary purpose is to free a cutter from the weakside or to force a switch by the defensive team. Anytime there is a switch it must weaken the defense at least psychologically.

We use this on the weakside exchange rule to free a forward, who will move out to guard, from denial defense. Its other major use in the passing-dribbling game is to free a wing man to cut through the open lane for either the jump shot or a driving lay-up.

3. The Vertical Rub-Off. We use the vertical rub-off when we use the point offenses or when we have a two guard front and wish to let the strongside forward set a blind pick. Its purpose is to free a cutter whose break goalward is perpendicular to the baseline. The pick that the cutter uses is a blind pick; and therefore, to be legal, must be set at least a full step away from the cutter's defender. It is the cutter's responsibility to dip and change directions, running his man into the blind pick.

Not only is there the additional option of the pass to the vertical cutter, there are also the many options of the blind pick. The shuffle cut is an example of the vertical rub-off.

4. The Lateral Rub-Off. The lateral rub-off is a parallel cut along or near the baseline. Pete Newell's Reverse Action Continuity, for example, uses this horizontal cut. It frees a cutter near the basket for the easy lay-up.

The lateral rub-off is a blind pick set near the baseline and near the lane for a weakside attacker to run his man into. The cutter has sole responsibility to dip his man into the blind screen.

5. The Multiple Screen. This is more than a three men game: at least four, two screeners and a cutter on the weakside and the ball handler on the strongside. When we set this screen, regardless of the number of screeners involved, we want them stacked along the lane, shoulder to shoulder, facing the basket. It is up to the cutter to run his man into the screen by influencing one direction and breaking the other.

If there is no switch and the cutter has run a good route, we can get him the ball for a high percentage shot. If there is a switch, we operate in two different manners. Upon hearing "switch," we sometimes allow the attacker whose defender has switched to break the opposite direction of high or low that the cutter took. Or sometimes we will have the attacker whose defender has switched screen for another member of the multiple screeners and have him break goalward. When we are operating under the last rule, we have the first cutter continue outside to the corner. There is usually so much confusion on the defense's part that the man who breaks goalward is open for the lay-up.

We run these multiple screens against the zones as well as against man to man. And, unless we are in our patterned phase of the passing-dribbling game, we run these screens at various and intermittent intervals. When the defense cannot guess the interval, they have more trouble defensing the multiple screens. In Chapters 7, 8, and 9 we will show all our patterns that make use of these multiple screens.

SUMMARY

After developing the individual fakes and cuts of our offensive system, we teach our two and three men games, using two on two and three on three drills until they are mastered. Then we teach the rules of the passing-dribbling game so that the offense will have complete team unity and continuity. But if the reader has one weak player, drill him on that weakness until he performs it well before teaching the last half of this text.

If the players are not developed individually, by two's, and lastly by three's, they will perform the following rules as robots. And if the coach wants his team to be mature, thinking players, who possess abundant savvy about the game of basketball, he does not want mechanical men.

CHAPTER 6

The Passing-Dribbling Game:

Secrets of
Its Rules and Automatics

Passing-dribbling games differ from coach to coach. Each has his own ideas and his own set sequences of cuts.

All offenses, to a degree, incorporate the same ideas, whether set-patterned, free-styled, or passing-dribbling. Each coach drills his squad on the offensive techniques and part plays he intends to use. Good coaches know that gimmick offenses will not win consistently, that well taught fundamental ones, such as the passing-dribbling game, will. Because of the new defenses invented daily, forcing coaches to teach too many patterns for players to learn adequately, the passing-dribbling game is the offense of the future.

Each year, regardless of the maturity of our players, we reteach the fundamentals of the one, two, and three men games before progressing to team offense. It is possible to begin with the rules presented in this chapter after having the passing-dribbling game installed for at least one year, and develop the one, two, and three men plays as the season advances. However, reviewing the basics of the passing-dribbling game before teaching the rules pays higher dividends.

Drills shown in this text develop timing, the most singularly important aspect of team offense. So far, we have developed the timing and knowledge needed for one, two, and three men offenses of the passing-dribbling game. Now we expand into a continuous five man offense.

But from this page on, the offensive system differs from any heretofore presented. The coach is going to let his players play and yet retain extensive control over their movements. The players will make their decisions instantly, and a good or bad season will result in direct proportion to how well the players have been taught to think. We can understand the missed shot, the lost ball, the physical error; but we will not tolerate the mental mistake. The first time, it is the player's error; the second time, the coach fails.

INITIAL GROUP STRATEGY FOR
THE PASSING-DRIBBLING GAME

We do not run our entire offensive system against every defense. There are those part plays that work best against man-to-man and those that work best against the zones. Many work equally well against both. At the initial chalk talk, we inform our players, not just the quarterbacks, which offenses we want against which defenses.

Against the Zones and Combinations Defenses

1. All the individual moves. Each man must be able to take advantage of all defenders, even when matched up one on one in a zone. Against most zones, the players will have to pull up short and take the jump shot.
2. The penetration drill. The reader will be surprised, if he has not tried it, how easy it is, after a few passes, to split two zone defenders, drive between them, and when the driver is stopped, lay the pass off to the vacated area for an easy lay-up.
3. All the two men cuts. Cutting through a zone is an easy way to get someone open, especially if the second cutter breaks into the vacuum created by the first cut. A cutter hunting a hole in a zone is comparable to a football player running to daylight.
4. All three men plays which take place away from the ball.
5. Posting. Against zones, we limit posting to the tall inside men. Any team can penetrate the zone by passing if they are patient enough. And after receiving the ball inside, the attacker must operate quickly, confidently, choosing his options wisely.
6. The lob pass option. It is very easy for a good leaper to get behind the back line of a zone, hold that position for a lob pass and a lay-up.
7. The backdoor option. Zone defensive men, as a rule, are vulnerable to all sorts of backdoor cuts. It is easy, for example, to drive vertically toward the baseline, be picked-up by an inside defender, cut a teammate backdoor along the baseline, break a tall man high inside to freeze the defensive center, bounce pass to the backdoor baseline cutter for a lay-up.
8. The formations. We like to put our attackers in the holes of the original zone alignment, but we have a few formations that we run against all zones: 12 tight, 14 high and low, A. Against the even guard front, we run 12 spread and 13. Against the odd guard front, we run 23. One of our favorite avenues of attack is to call two formations, like 14 low into 14 high

against 2-3 zones, creating openings as the players break from one alignment to another.

Against the Man to Man Defenses

1. All individual moves.
2. The penetration drill.
3. All two men plays, including the cuts.
4. All the three men plays, including the split the post series.
5. Everyone posts all exaggerated mismatches. It is not limited to just the big men.
6. The lob pass and backdoor options.
7. The formations. We run the formation that takes advantage of the defensive weaknesses. They change from team to team. The coach will have to recognize which defender is weakest, and then deploy his men in the manner that best exploits that weakness.

We never conduct chalk talks during practice. Practice time is precious. Chalk talks are held early in the morning so that players can spend the day absorbing and digesting the content. We do require that notes be taken and studied.

FUNDAMENTAL RULES

At our second chalk talk, we explain the fundamental rules of the passing-dribbling game. Interpreting these fundamental rules in advance of teaching the basic rules, while we are still developing the one, two, and three men games, sets the stage for complete offensive team development of this unique system.

1 No Two Attackers Cut to Same Spot at Same Time. Timing is an offensive essential. The second cutter is responsible for timing his cut so that he will arrive after the first cutter has had his opportunity. It is better to break too late than too early. Although two cutters should not reach the same area at the same time, it happens occasionally. When it does occur, the second cutter makes a V cut out of the congested area. This not only will take the second cutter out of the play, but it removes his defender and keeps both attackers in motion, creating more adjustments for the defense.

When three players break to the same spot, it can be turned into an offensive blessing. Each cutter, after setting for a count, V cuts in three different directions, creating cross-screening possibilities, making it impossible for the defense to cover all three cutters.

2. Anytime a Player's Motion Stops, He Will Be Benched. Players who remain motionless are hindrances to team offense. Even if a player is an All-America, he is hurting his team: his defender is able to help out on all other potential scorers. Players who stay in motion the entire game tire their defenders, defeating them consistently in the fourth quarter.

Conditioning, as stated previously, is a primary tenet of great offenses. Players who cannot stay in condition cannot play top-flight basketball. We do not subscribe to the theory: "if you want to rest, rest on offense." We believe that if you want to rest, rest on the bench.

3. The Dribble Must Be Kept Alive Between Any Ball Handler and Two Attackers. This is our way of informing our players that if they are going to dribble, they had better have a purpose for it. And we can think of only two legimate reasons for dribbling: on an individual clearout move or to set up the dribbling game, the weaves. So we always say look for someone to pass to, drive using the dribble, or shoot in that order. Indoctrinating this principle eliminates the futile and frustrating one bounce habit.

Coupling fundamental rule number 3 with fundamental rule number 4, the dribbler would have a purpose when he placed his dribble on the floor. If, as in rule number 4, the dribbler's teammate clears, we expect the one-on-one performer to complete his maneuvers within two dribbles. If, however, the dribbler's teammate breaks toward the dribbler, then we expect the weaving game to begin.

4. When Dribbling Toward a Teammate, That Teammate Must Clear the Area or Break Toward the Dribbler. If the teammate is clearing the area, the dribbler can either operate one on one or pass backdoor to the cutter who is clearing out. Cutters who dip and break toward the dribbler, put into operation the dribbling game, particularly the weaves.

BASIC RULES

The passing-dribbling game is a sophisticated, scientific attacking system based upon letting the players do at any particular moment whatever it takes to beat their defender. Players do not have to wait for a prescribed moment; they may cut when their defender is at his weakest. But they must break within the framework of the basic rules. The basic rules, which give an order or sequence of cutting, guarantee continuous concerted team movement.

Two different sequences comprise the basic rules: the listed order and the inverted order. The listed order begins with the perimeter attack, progressing to the inside; the inverted order starts with the inside assault and moves outside. On nights when we are stronger than our opposition inside, we commence with the inverted sequence. On all other nights we open with the listed arrangement, believing that good defensive teams prefer to prohibit inside offensive operations.

1. Strongside Guard Cuts First. Having this guard cut to the baseline on his first trip downcourt will determine the opponents defense. Running this cut first against opponents who change defenses each possession eliminates any confusion to the offense. This does not stereotype the strongside guard's movement because he has five different routes he can take and eight different methods of getting into the offense *(Chapter 5)* and eight formations from which he can run these five cuts. The strongside guard has a few guidelines to help him make his choice. He should choose the cut that will damage the defense the most. Two wrong choices results in his removal from the game.

The strongside guard position might be run by a guard, a forward, or a center. The same is true of the other positions. The rules apply to whoever happens to be in that area of the court, not to a particular person. The first two men down floor are the guards, the next two are the cornermen, and the last is the center.

His first decision is whether to cut through to the baseline or cut in some other direction. His initial cut of the game is always to the baseline, exhibiting the opponents defense. If the strongside guard's defender follows him, it is man to man; if his defender releases him to another guard, it is a zone.

The strongside guard should always cut completely to the baseline when facing a two guard zone front. From there he should go baseline strongside if he is having a good shooting night or if the offense wants to overload the strongside. If the offense wishes to utilize a baseline screen, the strongside guard would want to go weakside, and the ball would be reversed for the jump shot over that screen.

When facing a man to man defense, the strongside guard's decision would rest heavily on two factors. First, is he bigger than his man. If so he should cut to baseline at the foul lane and post. As long as the guard stays at the low post, the center would not follow his rule of becoming the second cutter for that would put two attackers in the same area. Secondly, is the center using the guard's cut as a temporary screen to get himself free. And if he is, are the center and strongside forward having a good offensive efficiency ratio. If so, the guard should cut baseline weakside. If this center and forward can cooperate with the strongside guard on the splitting series, the strongside baseline cut is a good move. If the center is an excellent screener, the guard's weakside cut offers a golden opportunity for the forward and center to use the strongside two men plays. But we do not want any cut overdone because the defense would adjust shortly.

Should the strongside guard choose not to cut baseline, he must either go to the pass or away from it. He should frequently go to the pass if he has a smaller man on him. This gives the guard a chance for a return pass from the forward, calling the go behind *(Chapter 8)*. If the guard's defender switches, the forward posts low. If there is no switch, the forward clears to the weakside. The guard has half a court to go one on one, or he can wait for the second cutter, the center, to break and screen for him. These two can cooperate on the screen and roll, blast, or if there is a switch the center posting the defensive guard low.

The strongside guard can choose to cut away from the ball when facing any zone defense or any double-teaming man to man. He should cut away from the ball when the center is having little or no trouble freeing himself with his individual inside moves or when the center is successfully head-hunting on the weakside (this would create a double-screen on the weakside set by the guard and the center). Cutting to the weakside is also the best option when any strongside teammate badly outsizes his man. These options get the inside high percentage shot by different players, keeping them all happy.

When this strongside guard has a small man on him, he could go away and screen for a bigger teammate, forcing an exaggerated mismatch. Posting this mismatch low produces an easy two points.

The last of the five strongside guard's options is to pass the ball, stand still, and let his teammates cut. This is the best move when all his teammates are capable of beating their men with inside one on one moves. This is also good when the strongside guard is an excellent outside shooter. His defender will probably sink to help inside. A simple pass back gets the strongside guard the uninterrupted twenty-footer. This not only gives us two points, but it psychologically causes the opponents to pressure more outside, openning up the inside game.

2. Center Gets the Second Option. Centers must know the options of the strongside guard. The center must read the actions of the strongside guard and act accordingly. He cannot, as the second cutter, break into an area that is occupied by the guard, the first cutter.

Once having read and considered the actions of the first cutter, the center has three options that he initiates. He has strongside choices, weakside alternatives, or he can head-hunt or go one on one.

If the center is stationed on the side of the penetrating pass, he is involved in his strongside selections. His first move is to set a pick for the strongside guard's first cut. He will follow this strongside guard into the low post area as soon as the guard has cleared. Should the guard not use the pick but go away from the strongside, the center would try his buttonhooks to get free low. However, if the guard chooses to cut behind the man he passed to, the center would come high and set a screen for the cutting forward and later for the guard, trying to set up a mismatch on a screen and roll.

The center can, at any time, choose to go away from the ball and exercise his weakside preferences. When facing a zone and the guard cuts baseline strongside, the center would move from side to low post. This would create an overload situation with three or four (depending upon the other guard) attackers on the ball side of the floor. Yet the ball would be at a high wing position where it could quickly be reversed to the other side of the floor creating another overload. The other weakside attacker is concentrating on rebounding.

As a penetrating pass comes into the cornerman, the center who is stationed on the weakside has several options. If the guard has cut baseline and goes to the strongside, the center can set a pick for one of the weakside men. The center should be facing the ball, letting the cutter set his man up for the pick. Or the center can break strongside for a pass and individual maneuvers or a split the post series. If the first cutter cuts baseline weakside, the center can use him for a screen and break strongside for a pass. Now the cornerman and the center can work a two men play, emphasizing the blast. Or the center can remain at the weakside position setting a double-screen with the guard for the weakside cornerman or the weakside guard. The center could get involved in the weakside plays and let the strongside cornerman operate one on one against his defender.

If the guard chooses to cut to the pass, the center should come strongside to screen for the cornerman, who will use him for either a jumper at the foul line or for a posting move low. If neither of those options are available, the center and guard can work their two men maneuvers.

Should the guard pass and go away, it usually means the center is capable of beating his man with inside moves. So the center should go strongside. If a teammate is also beating his man inside, the center can pick for that teammate.

The center has an option independent of how the guard cuts: the center may head-hunt at any time he wishes, To head-hunt the center sets a positive screen for any teammate on or off the ball. This screen is set just short of contact and within the visible range of the defender being screened. Its purpose is to force the switch creating confusion for the defense. If the cutter should happen to be open, that is an added advantage.

An automatic rule, discussed in a later section, tells our center and his teammates how to react when the center receives a penetrating pass during any of his maneuvers.

These options must be known and easily read by all players because the center position might be played by a guard or a cornerman. Whoever is the last player down floor on the fast break will be the center; and many times the center will get involved in weakside maneuvers and either a guard or a forward who thought he had his man beaten has used an individual cut into the center position.

3. The Weakside Has the Third Option. Weakside players have two primary responsibilities. First, they must keep their man busy and out of the strongside play. This is usually accomplished by simply exchanging positions, in which there can be a screen set by the option of the outside player. In this exchange the outside player always breaks on the inside.

Because most rebounds carom to the opposite side of the shot, the weakside's other primary responsibility is the offensive rebound. If this weakside attacker is having difficulty getting around his man, he should clearout his area so the other weakside attacker can get the rebound. He has two ways to accomplish this. He can exchange again, or he can go screen for the other weakside attacker.

There should be no weakside exchange against zones. The tallest or best rebounder should stay as the cornerman against zones.

After examining their two primary duties, weakside men are ready to enter into the passing-dribbling game. Before considering their movements or cuts, the weakside men must always provide an avenue to reverse the ball. The ball is reversed frequently against all zones and against all exaggerated man-to-man sags.

Weakside players become strongside players and, therefore, have no need for weakside maneuvers under two conditions. If the strongside guard passes and cut opposite without going baseline, this is the weakside guard's key to break baseline strongside or baseline then go weakside. In other words, the weakside guard assumes the options of the strongside guard. The center can also send a weakside attacker into a strongside position by choosing to go to the weakside or by setting a pick on the free throw line for a weakside cutter. The center keys the setting of this pick by spreading his legs and raising both arms as though he is going to rebound. This positioning serves a double purpose: not only does it key the weakside cutter, but it gives us two excellent offensive rebounding positions should the strongside player shoot. The cutter by virtue of movement has excellent rebound position and the center with his hands already up and ready.

Weakside players are free to screen for each other, to cut anytime they gain an advantage on their defender pursuant to the fundamental rules, to run any three men plays. They must, however, become strongside men when the original strongside calls such a move.

There is also one time that they must cooperate in a weakside double-screen. That occurs when the strongside guard passes and cuts behind the receiver. This cut calls the go behind, one of the passing-dribbling game's basic formations *(Chapter 8)*. The other strongside alignment creats the overload *(Chapter 7)*.

4. Inverting the Rules. The passing-dribbling game inverts its rules in two different orders and for two different reasons. Beginning with the center making the first cut *(rule 2)*, advancing to the guard's cut *(rule 1)* indicates the inside men can dominate their defenders. The second inversion commences operations whenever the cornermen can control their defenders. This inversion proposes for the weakside to cut first *(rule 3)*, going to the center option *(rule 2)* before permitting the guard cut *(rule 1)*.

There are four other possible associative orders, but these two sequences present the passing-dribbling game with the most effective inside-outside attack that is possible in the game of basketball. Coaches decide the array before each game.

Inverting the rules also gives the passing-dribbling game another look, causing scouts to think it has several more patterns. It makes the passing-dribbling offense more versatile, harder to scout, and most difficult to defend.

5. Adding Rules to Suit Unique Personnel. This requires exceptional judgment on the coach's part. He must first recognize the unique talent that his players possess, and then he must devise a workable rule that will not upset the delicate balance of his offense.

Many teams have a player who can shoot but do little else. This player should be placed at weakside guard, weakside cornerman, or strongside guard. The change in the rule would depend on positioning of the great shooter. If he is a weakside guard, then the rule should force him to the point regardless of who cuts when. If he is at strongside guard, then a rule forcing the weakside guard to cut first would be profitable. If he is a weakside cornerman, then the weakside exchange should be the first move. All these rule changes would place this great shooter outside, forcing the defense to spread, openning up the inside game.

There are those players on each squad who "are as wide as they are tall." These players make great screeners for freeing good shooters, and the rules should encourage this screening activity. The simpliest way to use this screener is to place him at center and run only the go behind.

Situations and talents are different on every ball club. There is no way to describe all of them. A coach should list the uniqueness of each of his players. He should then burn the midnight oil figuring some way of incorporating these unique qualities into his offense. Almost all the basic characteristics of great players have options within the framework of this passing-dribbling game.

6. On All Ball Reverses, the Weakside Cuts First. As the ball is being reversed, the old strongside is becoming the weakside. This new weakside man is to be the first cutter. This cutter can break off a double-screen or a single screen, depending upon the cuts in the first two rules.

If the strongside guard cuts strongside baseline, there will be three players on the strongside: the cornerman, the guard, and the center. If the center is on the big block when the ball is reversed, the baseline guard breaks off this center's blind pick. If the center is above the big block, the cornerman runs a lateral rub-off move. In the latter case the strongside guard could have moved to the free throw lane and set a double-screen with the center. The cornerman should dip before breaking around the double-screen.

The rules could also be inverted for the first reversal of the ball. To adhere to that inversion, the center would break first as the ball is moved from strongside to original weakside.

If there are only two players on the original strongside, then the first cutter has cut weakside. So the first and only cutter on the reversal would be the cornerman who would use the center for a lateral rub-off. But if we inverted the listed order, the center would be the only cutter, and his would be an individual cut.

Putting this rule into the passing-dribbling attack assures continuous play. And continuity is extremely important to all team offenses. Coupling this rule with the first three guarantees the passing-dribbling coaches that the basic cuts and moves of this unique offense can be run, re-run, and run again during any possession.

AUTOMATIC RULES

Besides the fundamental and basic rules, five automatics are employed when the defenses offer certain types of resistance. Obeying these five principles allows the passing-dribbling game to adapt instantly and automatically to defensive adjustments.

1. When Center Is Fronted, Clear Weakside. The overload formation positions a cornerman at strongside wing position, a guard at the strongside baseline, and the center at a side post position strongside. This leaves only two attackers to clear out the weakside when the defense fronts the side post. To obey this axiom the weakside guard clears to a point position and the weakside cornerman breaks either to high post in the center of the lane or to a high side post at the free throw line extended. The techniques of the center in receiving the high lob pass when fronted is discussed in Chapter 4.

The choice made by the weakside cornerman keys another two basic movements out of the passing game provided no attempt is made to throw the lob pass. If the weakside cornerman breaks to high post, he sets a blind pick for the point guard to cut backdoor. If he breaks to the high side post the guard utilizes an individual backdoor cut as the pass comes into the side post. These two cuts are used against all zone defenses as well as man to man because it gives the offense an exaggerated overload. From this alignment it is easy to reverse the action into an overload on the opposite side of the court *(see Chapter 7)*.

2. Clear Strongside When One-On-One Man Has an Advantage. As the game progresses, coaches determine when attackers can consistently defeat their defenders with individual moves. These men may or may not be the best individual attackers. The two best one-on-one attackers, for example, may have extremely talented defenders on them while the third best attacker may have a very weak defensive man. It is a coaching decision.

There are several ways to clear the strongside. If the individual attacker is a cornerman, the strongside guard passes to him and runs a give and go, clearing the strongside. The center remains on the weakside. If the individual attacker is a guard, he calls the go behind, leaving the center on the weakside. Or the first two basic rule cuts are run, and the ball is reversed, making sure that the weakside attacker is the best one-on-one man. All cutting stops momentarily giving the weakside man time to operate. Or the weakside cornerman can break to the side post; and when the ball is reversed to the point guard, the guard will have half of the court for his individual maneuvering.

Centers can get involved in clearouts by exchanging positions with the other players. Or a center can break to the ball, using the guard's give and go maneuvering as a screen. When the center breaks to receive the pass from the high cornerman, he must continue outside until his defender is on his back. When the cornerman passes inside, he runs the blast and clears to the weakside. Now the center has half a court isolated.

Not only does the coach determine when and who is the best individual attacker for that one game, but the passing-dribbling game has two conditions when its players immediately and automatically go into these one-on-one clearouts. Anytime a defender has three fouls on him before half-time or anytime a defender receives a fourth foul, that defender should be forced into one-on-one coverage before his coach removes him.

3. Post All Exaggerated Mismatches. Whenever a smaller defender covers an offensive player, that attacker activates an individual cut to the strongside low post, being careful not to cross with any other attacker. All other offensive players observe the defense on this posting player, apply the rules, and operate accordingly.

   4. The Sequence for Completed Passes into the Pivot. On completed inside passes, the pivot exploits his individual moves first. If it appears that this post man will gain no advantage, only one dribble permitted, the splitting series begins. After a few seconds, if no openning occurs, the pivot passes back outside.

   This inside man need not necessarily be the center. It can be anyone in the post position. Letting this attacker go one-on-one initially corresponds with all the other basic and fundamental rules. However, the center must never drive into the lane without shooting. So if he begins his fakes and cannot find an advantage, he does not put the ball on the floor. Rather, he pivots back outside. During this, the outside men have been dipping, preparing to split. Should all their splitting maneuvers be stopped, which is unlikely, a cutter will stop quickly, push off his front foot, break outside for a pass, and begin another sequence.

   5. Staying in Motion by Individual Cuts. Defenders make mistakes, errors in judgment that give a smart cutter an advantage. The passing-dribbling attacker is free to cut goalward anytime his defender makes a mistake. The attacker uses the individual cut that the defender dictates, but he must also stay out of the flow of the option called for by the basic rules.

   This means that the cutters must recognize the defensive mistakes as they are made *(see Chapter 5)*. And the cutters must fully remember the rules of this chapter so that no two men will break to the same spot at the same time.

FUNDAMENTAL THEORIES AND PRINCIPLES
OF THE PURE PASSING GAME

   When we run the pure passing game,, we do not want any screening on the ball. This would require the passer to use the dribble to set up himself or the screener. We want the pass then go screen opposite.

   We never want more than two dribbles regardless of the situation. If a player cannot score in two dribbles, then the teamwork of the pure passing game degenerates into a one-on-one confrontation. We want the two dribbles used primarily to set up the next pass.

   A player who is not involved in either passing or receiving the ball must move to the ball or away from it. In moving away from the ball, the attacker should screen. In moving toward the ball, a cutter should dip and use a screen. We prefer for the strongside to move away from the ball and for the weakside to move toward the ball. The passer must always pass and screen opposite or break on the give and go. The passer must never stand still after making a pass.

   When running the pure passing game, at least two and at most four passes (although a team can take more and we prefer three) should be required before a shot can be taken. In the pure passing game, the point player must make three screens before he can come back toward the ball. If a wing player passes to the corner, that wing player must screen for four players before reentering the pattern. And all screens in the pure passing game must be away from the ball. These screening rules assure the passing game of movement. And it forces teamwork.

After running the initial strongside guard cut and the weakside exchange and without the center choosing the second option, the players positions will be as shown in *Diagram 6-1*. When the center does not follow the rules of the passing-dribbling game by being the second cutter, it keys our offense into the pure passing game.

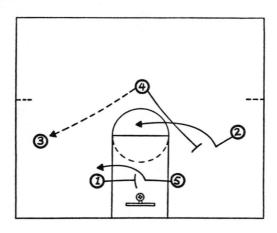

Diagram 6-1

Our pure passing game must not be confused with our regular passing game. In our regular passing game, we try to stay in an Overload alignment; in our pure passing game, we follow the rules given above in this section. We never permit dribbling in the pure passing game. This eliminates the penetration drill, reducing by one a massive means of scoring. Therefore we use both the regular and the pure passing games.

Patience must be exercised in the pure passing game. It is more methodical. We pass and pass and pass around the perimeter, screening inside until we can get a pass inside. The pure passing game is a spontaneous continuity of its own. Parts of the regular passing game can be incorporated into the pure passing game.

Diagram 6-1 shows the beginning of the pure passing game. 4 passes to 3 and goes to screen away. 4 must screen two more times before he can come back to the ball. 1, a guard, who is on the strongside goes to screen for 5, a center, who is a member of the weakside. The weakside comes to the ball, using the screens being set by the strongside, 4 and 1. If 3 can pass into 5, we have penetration; or if X1 switches off to 5, we have an initial mismatch. And these

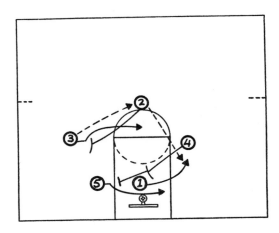

Diagram 6-2

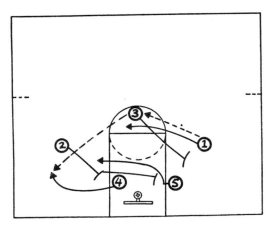

Diagram 6-3

passes adhere to our rule of three passes before a shot: 1 passed to 3 and broke to the corner, 3 passed to 4 while 1 moved inside, and 4 passed back to 3 to start the pure passing game.

When a small guard has broken inside, we like for the point man, 4, to pass back to 3. Such passing not only gives an inside mismatch, 1 screening for 5, but it assures 5, the big center, of staying inside throughout the continuity.

If 3 cannot pass inside, he passes to 2 *(Diagram 6-2)*. 4 screens down on 1, 4's second screen. 2 immediately hits 1, who pivots to check inside or takes a jump shot over 4's screen. 2 meanwhile goes to screen opposite. 2 was the point and therefore must screen three times before he gets back into movement toward the ball. After screening for 1, 4 screens for 5, completing his obligation of three screens before breaking back toward the ball. If 1 can pass inside to 5, he does. If 1 cannot hit 5, he passes to 3 and we reverse the passing game *(Diagram 6-3)*.

2 screens down for 4. If 4 can shoot the jumper, he does. If not, 2 sets his third screen away on X5. 3 meanwhile has gone to screen away for 1. 3 is now the point and must screen three times before reentering the play. If nothing develops inside, 4 reverses the ball to 1 and the pure passing game again changes sides of the court.

The pure passing game knows no boundaries. Its limits exist only in the minds of those who employ it.

Continuing Diagram 6-1, 3, instead of passing to 2, could pass to 5 in the corner. When a pass is directed into the corner, the wingman must screen for all four players before rejoining the attack. So 3 would go pick for 2 *(Diagram 6-4)*. 4, who was the point in Diagram 6-1, would be completing his second screen on 1. A bad defensive switch would give 4 a lay up.

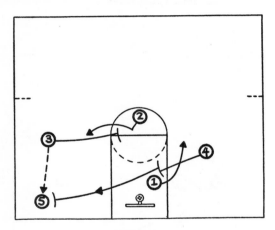

Diagram 6-4

Diagram 6-5 is an extension of Diagram 6-4. 5 passes to 2 who passes to 1 as 1 breaks around 3's second screen. 1 shoots the jumper if he has lost X1 on 4 or 3's screens. If 1 cannot shoot, he passes to 5 who broke around 4's third and last screen and 3's third and next to last screen. 5 could have the lay up or the short jumper. But if neither is present, 5 continues outside. 4 meanwhile has used 3's fourth screen. If either 5 or 1 (whoever has the ball) can get a pass inside to 4, it assures a high percentage shot.

After 1 hits 5, he, as point man, must screen three times before he again breaks toward the ball *(Diagram 6-6)*. 4, being on the strongside, must go screen opposite. 5 can pass to 2 reactivating Diagrams 6-1 through 6-3. Or 5 can pass into the corner to 3, beginning again the ideas displayed in Diagrams 6-4 through 6-6.

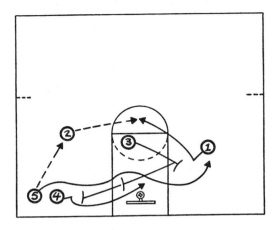

Diagram 6-5

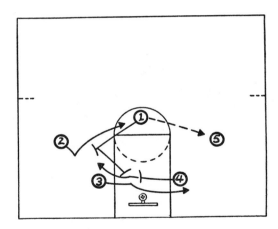

Diagram 6-6

Should the ball end up at the point and the point man be unable to pass to a wing man, the wing men on both sides screen down on the post men. This should always clear a passing lane. But should one still not be available, the point man could activate the penetration drill. Once he lays the ball off, the point man could again begin the pure passing game by beginning his three screens opposite.

Other part plays can be added to the pure passing game. For example, when 2 screens for 5 in Diagram 6-3, if X2 switches onto 5, 2 could reverse pivot and come back toward the ball. This move by 2 would put X5 on his back. A pass inside would give 2 the power lay up. We will leave it to the coach to devise other part plays to suit his personnel.

To get from the pure passing game into the Overload *(see Chapter 7)*, the strongside post man would break into the corner while the weakside post man would use an individual cut to the strongside. From Diagram 6-1, 1 would be in the corner and 5 would be the strongside post. With this minimal movement, all of the options of Chapter 7 become available. Transition, therefore, from the pure passing game to the regular passing game to the patterned offense is simple with little or no movement required by the players.

To get into the Go Behind *(Chapter 8)* from the pure passing game, the point man passes and breaks behind the pass receiver. In Diagram 6-1, 4 would pass to 3 and cut behind 3 for a flip pass back. 1 would still screen for 5; and 2, instead of breaking to the point, would set the weakside double screen with 1. Such movement by the point man keys the Go Behind. Transition was again simple. And transition from the Go Behind to the Overload and commutatively will be explained in Chapters 7 and 8.

It is equally as simple to get into the pure passing game from any of our eight passing-dribbling formations. It has been shown above from the single stack.

The 2-3 formation would operate exactly as the single stack with the strongside guard breaking to the corner and the center rolling all the way around to the weakside. All the point offenses, the 1-4 high and low, the "A" formation, the 1-2-2 tight or spread, the double stacks, and the 1-3-1, keep the two big men inside, the two wing men at wings, and the point at the point.

There are peculiarities that develop from each set. For example, the double stacks can start with screen downs. The team's alignment will look like Diagram 6-1, just different personnel in different spots. Most of those pecularities are obvious to the reader.

CHAPTER 7

The Passing-Dribbling Game:
Secrets of the Overload

Coaches should not expect players to always feel active. On certain days, athletes, like the rest of us, feel better and therefore perform better. On other days when they feel less than active, they move less. When those indolent days come, the passing-dribbling coach can bench his better players or he can force their movement with prearranged patterns. Our patterns not only follow the rules of our passing game, but they require all five men to move. Once action starts, reverting back to the rules of the passing game keeps the players in motion and it certainly provides more offensive versatility.

THE BASIC PATTERN

After following the initial passing game rule (strongside guard cuts first while weakside exchanges), 1, 2, 3, and 4 will end up in areas shown in *Diagram 7-1*. The center, 5, breaks to strongside adhering to the second passing game rule. This is the Overload, and it is reached after using these two cuts regardless of the basic formation employed. 3 now calls the patterned option by what he does with the ball.

Each attacker should recognize the team defense facing him. 1's inaugural cut supplies the answer. When 1 cuts from out front to the baseline, his man must either follow him, indicating man to man, or release him, revealing a zone.

All zone defenses, when the ball is in the corner, display the same skeleton (see section on zones later in this chapter). So the type of zone is really irrelevant. Besides, the Overload formation provides recurring triangles, even as the ball is moved from one side of the court to the other. And triangular positioning of players is the most acceptable method of defeating any zone. The Overload also furnishes excellent inside and outside men movement.

142

Man to man defenses are of two basic types: sag and pressure. It is easy for 3 to check the coverage on either 1 or 4 and determine the type of man defense (see strongside and weakside options, this chapter).

Zone or man, 3's primary check is inside. On the maiden trip downfloor 5 and 2 run a two men inside game. When facing a man to man or a zone, 5 and 2 roll, timing their movement so that one is leaving the strongside along the baseline as the other is arriving at the strongside high post. A straight zone defense cannot prevent one or the other from receiving a pass inside. An alert man defense might. But if we face man to man, 5 can screen for 2. If there is no switch, 2 will obtain the penetrating pass. If a switch occurs, 5 rolls back to the ball with X2 on his back. 5 now has posted X2, a smaller defender. Either way we get the pass inside.

If X5 fronts 5, 2 breaks to side high post, following the automatic rule: when center is fronted, clear weakside. Adhering to the mechanics of Chapter 4 will get 5 the lob pass lay-up.

RULES OF THE PASSING-DRIBBLING GAME
AS IT APPLIES TO THE OVERLOAD

Because we occasionally run patterns to create movement, it might appear that we leave our free-lance passing-dribbling game. But that is not true. Our patterns are set up to follow the rules of the passing-dribbling game. And, as in the section above, when patterned movement occurs, we will show how it conforms to the rules of Chapter 6.

SECRETS OF THE STRONG SIDE OPTIONS

Diagram 7-1 shows the end result of the strongside guard, 1, passing to the cornerman, 3, and breaking through on the give and go. Weakside guard 2 has exchanged with weakside cornerman 4. These two maneuvers follow the first basic passing game rule. Of course this is not the only method of getting into the Overload alignment; it is the simplest. Eight other entries were described in Chapter 5. Smart guards can originate infinitely more.

Nevertheless, 3 has the ball and his pass dictates our next team movement (this, too, follows the rules outlined in Chapter 6). 3 can pass to either 1, 4, or 5.

A pass inside to 5 calls four different options. 5 can work on his man one-on-one. 3 can cut off 5, running the blast. 3 can split the post with either 1 or 4. Or 3 can stand still or exchange with 1 or 4 while 5 pivots to face inside. During this pivot by 5, 2, or 4 if there were no exchange, would maneuver his defender on his back. A pass inside to 2 gets the high percentage shot.

While 5 has the ball, the outside perimeter men could run fake splits, or they

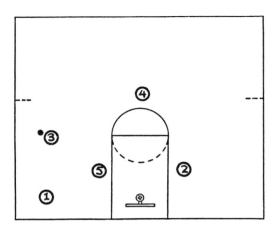

Diagram 7-1

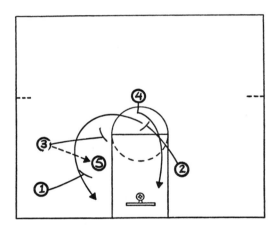

Diagram 7-3

could screen for each other, operating under the rules of the passing-dribbling game.

Diagram 7-2 exhibits the first of our several patterned strongside Overload options. As 5 pivots to face inside, after receiving pass from 3, 2 sets a blind screen for 4. If 4 is not open on his backdoor cut, he tries to position himself on the weakside for a strong rebounding position. Meanwhile, if the strongside has not split the post, 3 and 1 set spread double screens for 2 to cut around. Should none of these options net a shot, 4 positions himself weakside baseline, 3 relocates at the point, 1 situates at strongside wing, and 2 becomes the strongside baseline attacker. This emplacement again displays the Overload alignment.

Instead of passing inside to 5, the key that called the last option, 3 can elect

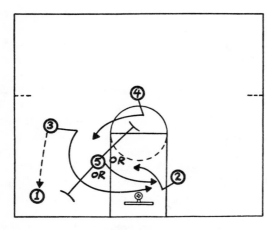

Diagram 7-2

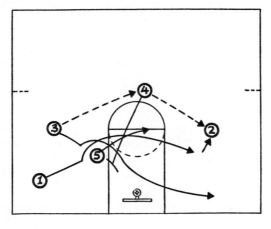

Diagram 7-4

to pass to 1, the strongside baseline man. 3 immediately clears an area for 1 to operate by running a give and go. 5 now considers three options: screen and roll with 1, screen for the point man 4, or effect a weakside double screen with 3. 5 will screen and roll with 1 if X1 is smaller than 5, if 1 is an excellent shooter over a screen, or if 1 plays the two men game with authority. He will screen for 4 if 4 can influence opposite and cut sharply to the ball, if 4 is taller than X5, or if 1 is an excellent one-on-one operator. 5 activates the double screen when we wish to run our Overload continuity (described next). Not only does this give 2 an opportunity to break off the double screen, but it guarantees continuous team movement.

3 can choose to pass to 4, calling the continuity. The continuity is used at

the end of each quarter, insuring us the last shot. Controlling the openning tip and getting the last shot of each quarter equals an additional possession each quarter. An extra possession each quarter is worth 16 potential points (the mathematical principle of basketball). Whenever we are stalling, we also make use of the continuity *(see Chapter 10)*.

After 4 receives the ball, he can immediately pass to 2, he can drive toward 2, activating the penetration drill, or he can fake a pass to 2 and have 2 cut backdoor for the backdoor or lob pass option. But if 2 receives the ball outside, 3 immediately runs a horizontal rub-off cut using 5's post pick. 1 follows with a cut around 4 and 5's double screen. 1 continues to high post strongside before sliding down into the low post. Should X5 switch onto either cutter, 5, who screened facing the ball, breaks toward the ball. If none of these options worked, 5 breaks around 4's screen down for the jumper or a pass back from 2 around to 4 and the continuity continues.

We sometimes alter this with an initial double screen for 3. When this happens 1 comes along the baseline, as the ball is being reversed, and sets a double screen shoulder to shoulder with 5. Upon seeing this, 3 influences baseline then breaks around the double screen. The rest of the continuity is the same as shown above.

If the coach has an excellent big man whom he wants to keep near the basket, 5 and 1 can exchange routes and responsibility. 1 would still be the second cutter, only he would look for the jump shot at the point position. 5 would be the third cutter, still around 4's screen, but he would cut to side high post.

Diagram 7-5 illustrates 4's calling off the continuity by passing to and breaking around 2. This keys the deadly blast between 4 and 2. 5 screens down on 1 and rolls. If X5 switches to 1, 5 gets the lay-up. If X5 does not switch, 1 gets the jumper. Remember X1 is a small guard and 5 is a foot taller center. If none of these options score, 4 sets up strongside baseline, 2 dribbles out to a high

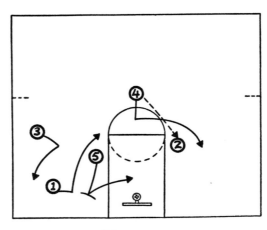

Diagram 7-5

wing, 1 stations at the point, 5 becomes the post, and 3 is the weakside attacker as the Overload alignment changes sides of the court.

Each pattern follows the basic rules of the passing game in the listed order. This makes it easy for us to switch from patterned play to passing game or commutatively. To add to the success of the patterned game we attach an automatic, which also follows the automatic passing game rule: when center is fronted, clear weakside.

When X5 fronts 5, 2 breaks to the high side post strongside. Of course, the first option, the lob pass to 5, is available, but that is the passing and not the patterned game. To continue the pattern game, getting five players in motion, 3 would hit 2. 4 watches X4. X4 will often cheat a glance toward the pass into 2. At that moment 4 backdoors for the pass and the lay-up. 4 can create his own backdoor by faking a split the post maneuver. When X4 moves on ball side of 4, 4 races hard toward the basket.

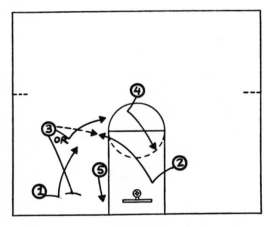

Diagram 7-6

Meanwhile, 3 has decided to either screen baseline for 1 or influence baseline and run the blast with 2. If 3 can beat his defender one-on-one, he would influence baseline. If 1 is better equipped to defeat his defender, we want the double screen by 3 and 5. If no score is immediate, 1 becomes the point, 4 the weakside, 5 strongside baseline, 3 the strongside wing and 2 the postman; and we continue the pattern or passing game.

SECRETS OF THE WEAKSIDE OPTIONS

When 4 receives the reverse pass from 3, he can call off the strongside continuity by his movement. Two changes have already been discussed: Diagram

7-5, the blast with the screen down and roll; and the backdoor, run mainly when 2 has denial pressure from X2.

4's third change is the give and go *(Diagram 7-7)*. He passes to 2 and either catches his man cheating glances at the pass or not jumping toward the pass. In either case, 4 breaks hard goalward for a return pass from 2 and the lay-up. If 2 does not pass to 4, 4 must decide to either cut weakside baseline or strongside baseline. Either way, 5 breaks toward the ball, utilizing individual inside moves to free himself for the penetrating pass. 3 screens baseline for 1, exemplifying exchanging on the weakside. 1 assumes the point and 3 the weakside. 2 is the strongside wing. 4 the strongside baseline, and 5 the post.

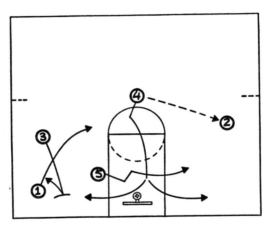

Diagram 7-7

4's next weakside option is to pass and screen on the ball *(Diagram 7-8)*. 4's screen on X2 should give 2 the area around the free throw line for one-on-one mechanics. 5 can either screen for 3 or 1; or 5 can use individual cuts across the lane. If 5 screens for 3 or 1, he becomes the new post man. If 5 uses individual inside maneuvers, 3 and 1 exchange.

2 could screen and roll for 4 as 4 receives the reverse pass. 1, 3, and 5's options in the weakside screen and roll, as the reverse pass screen and roll by 2 is called, is the same as in the pass and screen on the ball (Diagram 7-8).

The last weakside option, the pass and screen away from the ball, gives us some weakside double screen while clearing the strongside for one-on-one maneuvers *(Diagram 7-9)*. 4 passes to 2 and goes directly to set a screen on weakside. 5 has the option to break toward 2 for the two men game or to set double screens with 4. Whichever man 4 and 5 screen for cuts across the lane into strongside baseline. The other, 1 or 3, uses individual cuts to receive a pass inside. 5 breaks high to the point and 4 is the new weakside attacker. And we are again ready to run a weakside or strongside option off the Overload.

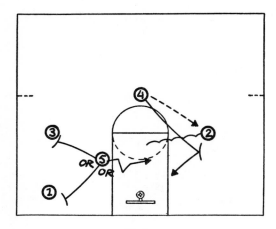

Diagram 7-8

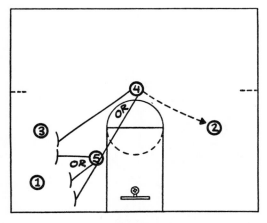

Diagram 7-9

THE OVERLOAD AGAINST THE ZONES

All zone defenses require that their players devote more attention to the ball instead of the attackers. All defenders occupy specific areas with definite coverage responsibilities. Offensive ball movement controls the zone's defensive shifts. Pressure is put on the man with the ball while all the other defenders reinforce the ball defender. Knowing that all zones operate under these principles helps us overload all zones in the same manner, keeping our zone offense versatile yet simple.

All standard zones have the same alignment when the ball is in the corner

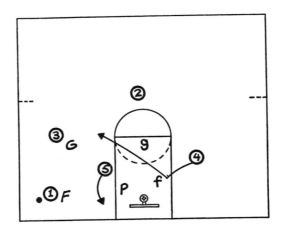

Diagram 7-10

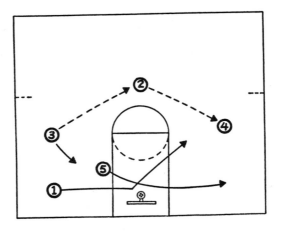

Diagram 7-12

(Diagram 7-10). Diagram 7-10 also displays the Overload after the initial cut by 1. Remember the weakside does not exchange against the zones. On our first trip downfloor, we run the inside roll. As 5 is leaving 4 is entering the strongside. This means that P must cover both 5 and 4 or get inside help from a guard, weakening the zone around the perimeter. Frequently, 1 and 3 pass as 5 and 4 roll. When 3 passes to 2, we run the high inside roll. 3 must be covered by G and 2 would be covered by g. As 4 rolls high across the lane, P cannot get there in time to cover the inside pass. So 3 has a clear passing lane inside to 4. 5 gets clear underneath for a pass from 4 or an offensive rebound.

On all ball reverses, the weakside cuts first, a basic rule, *(Diagram 7-11).* So

1 cuts across the lane to a high post. The center cuts next. 5 cuts low and can go across the lane to the corner if he chooses. However, if 4 can get the ball inside to 1, we want 5 breaking back under the basket, 4 breaking to corner strongside, and 3 breaking to free throw line weakside. From this position, an overload on original weakside, we can roll (Diagram 7-10) or continue to reverse ball until we get it inside or get the clear outside shot.

On some ball clubs, 1 is too small to operate effectively inside. In that case, we leave 1 on the weakside and send 3, a forward, inside.

A pass into the corner by 4 keys another movement *(Diagram 7-12)*. It is a simple outside roll. However, 2, 3, and 4 must recognize the zone confronting them. Without this recognition, those perimeter players would match up with the zone. And we prefer not to match up but to position the perimeter men in the holes of the zone. So 2 and 3 would greet a point zone with a two guard front. 2, 3, and 4 would simply fill the holes vacated as they roll against an even zone front. 1 and 5 would continue their inside movement. This creates long difficult slides for the zone defenders.

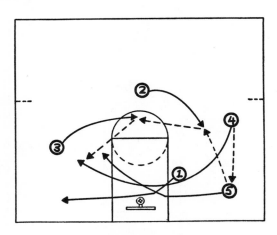

Diagram 7-11

4's pass to the corner keys either the inside roll or the outside roll. If 4 holds his position, then the inside roll begins; if 4 cuts through, the outside roll commences.

From the basic overload, a triangular attack, we revolve into a box or a diamond attack. *Diagram 7-13* shows the evolution into a box. It gives the appearance of the roll, but 3 and 1 stay, instead of constantly rolling. 4, 5, 1, and 3 pass the ball against three defenders until one of them is open for an easy jump shot. 4 can reverse the ball to 2 and we reestablish the box on the original weakside by breaking as in Diagrams 7-11 and 7-13.

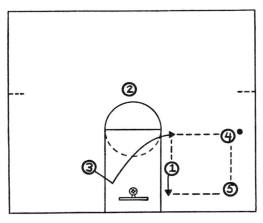

Diagram 7-13

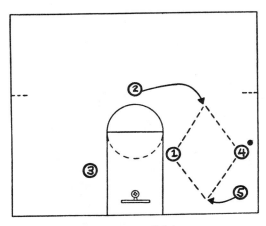

Diagram 7-14

Diagram 7-14 shows the creation of a diamond attack from the overload triangle. Again four men attack three with strongside passing until an easy jumper is available. We run the diamond as a strong outside shooting assault, and we run the box when we encourage a strong inside offensive. 1 tries to post his zone defender low. If 1 is a small player, he can roll out of the play, exchanging position with 3.

There are other patterns which we run against the zones. They are quick hitting plays, designed to get quick but unhurried shots. They will be presented in Chapter 9.

THE OVERLOAD FROM THE OTHER SEVEN FORMATIONS

There are many maneuvers that teams can use to move from their favorite starting alignment to the positioning described in Diagram 7-1. In this section we will show how we get from our basic seven formations into the Overload alignment *(Diagram 7-1)*. The reader must refer to Diagrams 1-3 through 1-11 as we develop those diagrams into Diagram 7-1.

From the single stack, Diagram 1-3, to the Overload, Diagram 7-1, there is no need for further discussion. This text has been developed from the single stack.

From Diagram 1-4, 14 high formation, 1 would pass to 2, cutting off 4 on a vertical rub-off cut. 4 would follow 1, staying at low post as 1 cuts to strongside corner. 5 would screen on weakside for 3. This weakside exchange puts 3 at the point and 5 at the low post weakside.

We also run quickies from these formations. 1 could use a screen by 4 and 5. When 1 gets his defender set up, he calls "swing," cueing the wing man to break backdoor to weakside. Then 1 drives off the center screen for the jumper or a lay-up. Some other quickies are obvious, and the reader can develop his favorites.

Let's let 1 pass to 2 *(Diagram 1-5)* in the 14 low formation. 1 then has option of breaking to strongside wing or setting a double screen with 5 for 3's cut. If 1 goes strongside, then 5 screens for 3. 3 is point man and 5 is weakside attacker. If 1 and 5 double screen, 3 breaks to strongside wing and 5 becomes point. While 1 is running the give and go to the weakside, 4 and 2 can play the two men game.

Diagram 1-6 displays the "A" alignment. This provides the same rotation as 14 high. However, there is the initial advantage of a screen down by either 4 or 5 and the weakside running the three play *(Diagram 5-19)*.

12 spread alignment *(Diagram 1-7)* provides many excellent quickies and many superb entrances into the Overload. 1 can either pass and screen on the ball or screen away. 1 can run the give and go. 1 can run the penetration drill. 1 can pass and cut away, leaving the strongside to two men operations. 4 and 5 can roll inside or screen for each other, activating the entire inside game. This formation can be a complete offense by itself for an entire season. If 1 passes to 2 and stays, for example, 5 can break strongside center and 4 strongside baseline, leaving 3 as the weakside attacker, or 5 can screen for 3, exchanging duties with him. There are many other entries into the Overload from 12 spread, but most of them are evident to the reader.

12 tight, shown in Diagram 1-8, supplies the passing-dribbling attack with additional quickies versatility. Of course, the same entrance into the Overload is available from this formation as in 14 and 12. But we have a pet beginning. 1 passes to 2 and goes screen for 3. Meanwhile, 4 screens for 5, and 5 continues to

strongside baseline. 3 then horizontally rubs his man off on 4. 1 goes back to the point.

13 admits uniqueness to the quickie entrance *(Diagram 1-9)*. As 1 brings ball down floor, 4 sets a blind pick on X5. 5 rolls to the basket for lob pass and lay-up. 1 can call this quickie with the word "popcorn." But getting into the Overload through the main gate requires 1 to pass to 2. During his dribble, however, he tries to set X1 up so that 5 can screen X1. 1 runs a give and go. 1 can cut baseline strongside or can screen for 4 who comes across lane to baseline strongside. 5 follows into side post and 3 fills point position.

If 1 passes to 3's side, the same cuts can occur, or 3 can pass to 4, and then 3 can set a screen for 5 to come around for the easy jumper.

Diagrams 1-10 and 1-11 illustrate the double stacks. The Overload can be achieved in the same manner as from the 12 and 14 formations. An added advantage, of course, is the immediate screen down for an outside jumper or an inside exaggerated mismatch.

CHAPTER 8

The Passing-Dribbling Game: Secrets of the Go Behind

While the Overload is a passing game, where dribbling is scarce, the Go Behind is a dribbling game, where passing is rare. Most coaches teach only the passing game, but it is easier to defeat some teams by the dribbling game. Although we prefer the passing game to the dribbling game, for the offense to be as versatile as possible, we have included the Go Behind.

THE BASIC PATTERN

In keeping with the format of this book, the Go Behind's basic pattern will be described in its entirety from the single stack formation. The Go Behind from the other seven alignments will be developed briefly in a later section in this chapter.

Diagram 8-1 exposes the key that calls the Go Behind and the initial two men movements. 1 passes to 3 and cuts behind 3 for a return pass. 1 should pass and influence toward the center of the court before breaking back toward 3. 1 should move within a few steps of 3, then dip as though he is going to run the give and go. Upon receiving the ball, 3 should face the basket as though he is going one-on-one. These actions by 1 and 3 keep their defenders from anticipating the play.

However, if X1 plays 1 in such a manner that 3 cannot pass back to 1, then 1 continues along the baseline, running 3's deep route.

If X1 is rubbed off onto 3, after the hand-off or flip pass, the forward, 3, should have a mismatch and would post low. If, however, X1 stays with 1 and X3 sags low to prevent 3 from buttonhooking low, 3 would pop out above 5's screen for a jump shot.

1 and 3 have the first two men options. They try to outsmart their defenders.

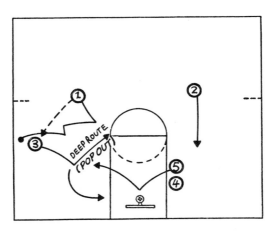

Diagram 8-1

3 can clearout, leaving 1 a one-on-one situation. 3 can screen, letting 1 shoot over the screen. 3 can hand the ball to 1 and quickly break goalward for a return pass. 3 can break hard goalward and then buttonhook into the low post position for a return pass and an easy inside move *(see Chapter 2)*. After exploiting these moves, 3 can go screen for 5 which marks the beginning of the third man in the play. 5 can then proceed to screen for 1, designating the beginning of the Go Behind's five man pattern.

After 1 and 3 try to outthink their defenders, 5 crosses the lane, working his inside maneuvers for a pass and an advantageous shot. If 1 or 3 should pass inside to 5, the two of them (5 and the passer) can run the blast. But if no pass comes inside, 5 screens and rolls with 1. X1 must defend 1 on his baseline side or at least toe to toe. Should 1 gain a step on the baseline, he has an unstoppable drive to the basket. This defensive positioning helps 5 set a near perfect screen for 1. 1 dribbles hard around 5 toward the basket. If X5 switches, 1 reverses and shapes up with 5, who has rolled posting X1 low, in a line of 45. If X1 fights over the top, 1 should have the jump shot. If perfect defense is played or if 5's screen was lazily set, 1 still has the middle of the court to perform one-on-one.

A change of part play (changing only a small portion of the original pattern) that we like gives 3 a lob pass for a lay-up. Instead of staying low, 4 breaks across the lane with 5, setting a double screen high. 2 comes to the point. 3 hands the ball to 1 and breaks around 4 and 5 for the lob pass and the lay-up *(Diagram 8-2)*.

Another change of part play pattern gives 5 the high percentage inside shot. Instead of 5 flashing across the lane to set the screen for 1, 5 stays at weakside low post. 3 hands off to 1 and then 3 comes to screen for 5. If 1 can hit 5 inside, he has an easy shot. Otherwise 1 could go one-on-one or wait for 5 to set the high pick. Should 1 decide to go one-on-one, 5 has the option of screening for him or

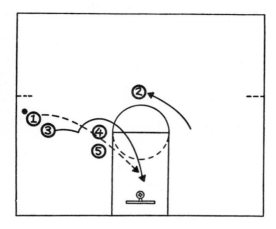

Diagram 8-2

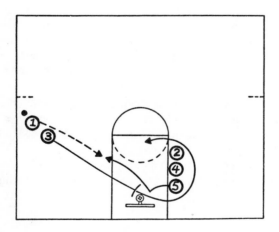

Diagram 8-3

letting 1 continue one-on-one. Once 1 picks up his dribble, 3 breaks around the double screen set by 2 and 4, and 5 goes across the lane on an individual flash pivot maneuver. When 3 receives the pass from 1, 5 moves outside and toward 1 several feet. 1 breaks off 5, manipulating a horizontal rub-off on 5. 1 continues around the double screen set by 2 and 4, and the offense continues the many options of the Go Behind *(Diagram 8-3)*.

Should there be no part play changes called, 1 has further option of passing to 3 who ran his man into a double screen *(Diagram 8-4)*. Or 1 can run the weaves by either dribbling toward 3 or reversing his direction and dribbling toward 5.

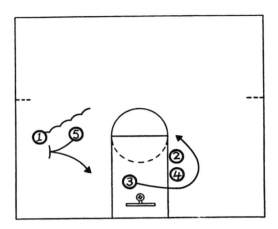

Diagram 8-4

We have many weaves which are pre-planned. The three man weave would include 1, 3 and 5 running the regular weave. The four men weave would permit 4 to utilize a screen set by 2 before getting into the flow. Or the five men weave would require that every man, after his dribbling hand-off, head hunt for another teammate.

If the offense is begun on the strongside, 2 would initiate the Go Behind by passing to 4. In this case 5 is already on the strongside trying to set his man up for an inside pass. All the other options of the basic pattern off the Go Behind are still available.

A pass is not required to begin the pattern. 1 could dribble toward 3, and 3 could run his deep route or his pop out. Thus we have a dribbling entrance into the Go Behind.

GETTING INTO THE OVERLOAD
FROM THE GO BEHIND

To be successful, patterned offenses must not require major movements by any player as the offense converts from one set pattern to another. Such movement would give the defense lull time, which they would use for regrouping. Our patterns, like our passing-dribbling game, move swiftly from one play to another without players having to readjust their positioning on the court.

Diagram 8-5, an extension of Diagram 8-4, shows 1's continuing his drive across the center of the court after 5 has set his screen and rolled. A pass from 1 to 3 followed by 4's popping out to the corner puts the offense into the Overload. Now we can run any option of the Overload *(see Chapter 7).*

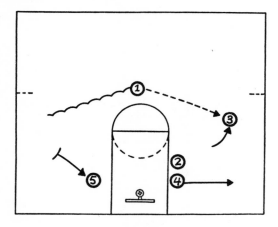

Diagram 8-5

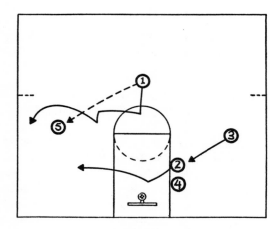

Diagram 8-6

GETTING INTO THE GO BEHIND
FROM THE OVERLOAD

Let's say that 1 reverses his direction, passes to 5, dips, and cuts behind 5 for the return pass *(Diagram 8-6)*. 2 becomes the new center, and he uses individual cuts as he breaks across the lane. 3 sets the double screen with 4. And we are back into the Go Behind.

Diagram 8-7, a continuation of Diagram 8-4, exhibits 1 passing to 3, breaking behind him, thereby calling the Go Behind. 4, who begins his break

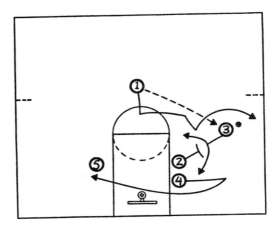

Diagram 8-7

into the corner as he would to create the Overload strongside, backdoors baseline
as 1 cuts behind 3. 2 breaks high, and the Go Behind begins again.

RULES OF THE PASSING-DRIBBLING GAME
AS IT APPLIES TO THE GO BEHIND

The first rule *(Chapter 6)* of the passing-dribbling game grants the strongside guard the lead option. The Go Behind begins with this strongside guard's
making a pass and breaking. He can go away and screen for the weakside guard,
who assumes the strongside guard's duties. He can cut through on the give and
go, again letting the weakside guard undertake the responsibility of the strongside guard. Or he can dip and break behind the pass receiver himself.

After the forward hands the ball back to the guard, the cornerman cuts
around the center who has moved from weakside to strongside on an individual
cut. The center, therefore, activates the second option.

The strongside forward has cut around a double screen set on the weakside.
That forward is now a weakside player. And he has the third choice regardless of
what weave or pattern we are in.

ALTERNATIVE PART PLAYS FROM THE GO BEHIND

Diagram 8-8 depicts the inside roll by the three big men 3, 4, and 5. Upon
seeing the roll, 2 dips back out front for floor balance. These three rollers have
four seconds to use individual cuts to free themselves from their defenders. If

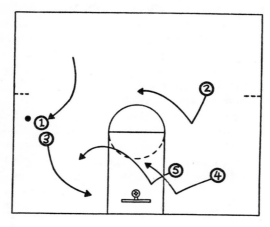

Diagram 8-8

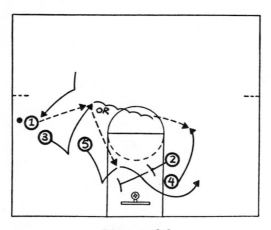

Diagram 8-9

unsuccessful, 1 can pass to 2, beginning another pattern; or 1 can dribble toward 2, activating the weaves.

Diagram 8-9 illustrates the pop out pass to 3. 3 should have the jumper with X3 being picked by 5. 5 should immediately go to the goal for an offensive rebound; but should 3 not shoot, 5 buttonhooks above his defender, who is probably trying to box 5 off the boards, for an inside pass and a high percentage shot. While 5 maneuvers in the lane, 2 screens for 4 who has a one-on-one move until 2 screens for 5. A good screen by 2 would get the smaller X2 off on 5. A pass by 4 to 5 gets the mismatched bucket inside. Anywhere along the line, 3, 4, or 1 can start the weaves.

An excellent alternative to the basic Go Behind has both guards breaking toward the ball followed by the 3 play on the weakside. Timing is most important for the success of this part play substitute. It begins as the regular Go Behind with 1 passing to and breaking behind 3. After 3 hands off to 1, he runs his regular high pop out route, pausing inside the free throw circle. This pause represents a rub-off blind screen for 2 to cut around. 1 can pass to 2 for the lay-up. 2 forces his guard to follow him into the strongside corner. After 2 cuts by the rub-off, 3 breaks to the point for a pass from 1. After 3 receives the ball, 5 screens down for 4, or 4 can use 5 as in the Cincinnati Swing and Go offense made famous by Ed Jucker. If 3 passes to 4, the latter has a jumper or a one-on-one move. 5 can come back toward 4 and shape up in a line of 45. Instead of passing to 4, 3 can pass to 5 who should have his defender or X4, depending upon the defensive coverage of X4 and X5 on the screen down, on his back *(Diagram 8-10)*.

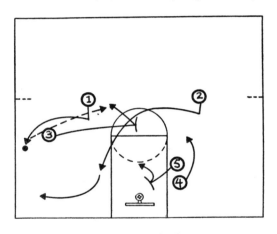

Diagram 8-10

THE GO BEHIND AGAINST THE ZONES

Regardless of the zone being faced, 1 passes to 3 and breaks behind 3, continuing into the corner. Should 3 misread the defense and hand off to 1, 3 would slide into the corner. 1 would call "slide," helping 3 recognize the defense. 2 cuts to the point position so the ball can be reversed. 5 comes high. If he is open, 3 or 1 hits him. If he is not open, 5 slides low and then breaks across the lane. 4 times his break high to correspond with 5's break low. Now we have an exaggerated overload, we have triangles spread throughout the zone, and we have an avenue to reverse the ball.

Instead of 1 passing and breaking behind 3, 1 could loop behind 3's defender. 3 could dribble toward center of the court, hitting 1 in the area just vacated by 3's defender.

Or 2 could break behind the zone into the corner while 1 fills 3's responsibility.

As 3 reverses the ball to 2, 4, who began his break low, rolls back high. Many times 2 can pass into 4 who can jump shoot or hit 5 or 3 on the baseline for an easy shot. Should 2 fail to hit 4 inside, he passes to 5 who has rotated outside. 2 breaks behind 5 into the corner. 3 and 4 roll inside, and 1 comes out high to provide a passageway for the reversal of the ball.

Of course 1 and 2 could again exchange duties. 1 could race baseline as ball is reversed. 1 could use 4 as a baseline screen, an extremely effective move against the 1-3-1 zone.

If a team runs the same zone each possession, we will call out the formation or formations which place our shooters in the holes of that zone alignment. Then we pass the ball around until an easy shot develops.

As the reader can see, the zone patterns are basically the same as in the Overload *(Chapter 7)*. Different methods of getting the zone attack started are employed from the Go Behind. The dribbling game is not used against zones. Dribbling only aids zones. It gives defenders time to recover their positions and protect their areas better.

THE GO BEHIND FROM THE OTHER SEVEN FORMATIONS

There are many maneuvers which teams can use to move from their favorite starting alignment to the positioning described in Diagram 8-1. In this section we will show how we get from our basic seven formations into the Go Behind alignment *(Diagram 8-1)*. The reader must refer to Diagrams 1-3 through 1-11 as we develop those diagrams into Diagram 8-1.

From the 14 high formation *(Diagram 1-4)*, 1 could pass to 2 and cut off 4 for a vertical rub-off. 1 continues to the weakside setting a double screen with 5. 4 and 2 work the two men plays. Or 1 could pass to 2 and cut behind 2. In the latter case 3 and 5 set the weakside double screen. 4 could choose at anytime to go screen for 5, letting 5 become the center. The same options are available from 14 low *(Diagram 1-5)*.

The A formation *(Diagram 1-6)* offers the same options as 14 high and low. But the A is also used to permit 1 to keep the dribble. 1 can use 4 and 5 to force a switch. When 1 calls "clear," he means for the low wing men to clear the side of the dribbler. Such as 1 tries to rub X1 off on 4. 2 clears that side. If 1 is successful and X4 does not switch, 1 has the lay-up. If X4 switches, 4 has small guard on him low. However, if good defense is played and X1 covers 1 and X4 plays 4, then 1 dribbles to high wing and 4 comes to screen for him while 2 has circled around the weakside double screen set by 3 and 5. Hence the Go Behind again.

12 spread or tight (Diagrams 1-7 and 1-8 offer other screening possibilities). 1 can pass to 2 and run the give and go, go behind, or screen opposite, getting 3

into the Go Behind. 2 can pass to 4 and screen for him, letting 4 become the dribbler. Or 2 can let 4 screen baseline side on screen and roll and then reverse his action back into the Go Behind. 3 and 5 would be setting the weakside double screen.

13 is set up for 1's pass to 2. 1 tries the vertical rub-off on 5. 5 goes to screen for 2 while 3 and 4 set the weakside double screen.

Diagrams 1-10 and 1-11 show the double stack alignment. Let's use Diagram 1-11 for explanations and let 4 screen for 2. 2 breaks high and 1 passes and goes behind. We like for 4 to go screen for 5, giving 5 an easy driving lay-up if there is a lapse in the defense. 3 and 4 set the weakside double screen and 1 and 5 operate the strongside two men game.

CHAPTER 9

The Passing-Dribbling Game: Secrets of the Quickies

Teams that drill on quickies can score quickly. And numerous times during a game teams strategically need that quick score. The quickie is to the offense what drawing the charge is to the defense.

Quickies should possess three primary characteristics: they should resemble the basic patterns as much as possible; they should deviate only one player drastically from his ordinary routes, thereby catching the defenders off-guard; and they should develop quickly where timing would be of utmost importance.

WHY USE QUICKIES

Coaches try everything to keep their players from developing staleness throughout the long basketball season. Physical vapidness results from a lack of mental freshness. Teaching a quickie or two, especially late in the season, relieves that mental staleness because anything new always intrigues and inspires players to perform better. By teaching a quickie or two for all ball games, a coach can practice without fear of being flat, even late in the year.

Quickies score easy baskets at strategic moments of a ball game. When a team has the ball and wants to take the last shot of a game or at the end of a quarter, when a basket is desperately needed, or when a basket would break the backs of the opponents are three examples of tactical importance. In the semi-finals of one state tournament, we had an eight point lead with one minute to go in the first half. We went to our quickie system and a full court press, stretching that eight point lead into fifteen by halftime. The game was ours; the opposition never played the second half with any enthusiasm.

Quickies teach attackers and defenders many variations of offenses and defenses. This aids developing informed, thinking basketball athletes.

Quickies can regain temporarily lost momentum. For example, we could have an eight point lead and our opposition could score three unanswered buckets. Two quickie scores sandwiched between a changing aggressive defense could retrieve that lost impetus.

Forcing the opposition into another defense is a stratagem for quickies. For example, a team might be playing man-to-man. We commence our quickies which scores three or four quick baskets. The opposition takes time out and switches to a zone.

Quickies can serve as rewards to players who have had an excellent practice week. Players practice hard in hopes that they will get a quickie on Friday night. It becomes a matter of pride, bandied by the players daily. Usually the player naving a good practice week has the great Friday night game. Rewarding him with a quickie also benefits the team. A player who does not have great offensive ability but does play considerably because of his rebounding or his defense can and should be rewarded with a quickie against a weak opponent. But never let the team know who the weak opponents are. Let the non-offensive player think he earned the quickie. Quickies build pride and team morale.

Defensive players who think and challenge every offensive action on the court fall easy prey to the hard hitting terminal quickies. Against tremendous pressure, quickies work wonders, discouraging such pressure defenses. And more and more coaches have begun teaching more and more pressure defenses.

Quickies offer a change of pace from the ultra patterned styles of play. Such change ups, used discreetly, can disrupt even the most sophisticated defense. And in the passing-dribbling game, it offers the patterned coach more control over his offense.

QUICKIES AGAINST MAN-TO-MAN

Quickies work best against man-to-man defenses. They can force unpoised coaches into a zone very quickly.

The coach should evaluate his material and the personnel of his next opponent before choosing which options he would want to stress for that game. Suppose the opposition has weak defenders at guard and the attackers have at least moderate offensive guards. The coach would want to make use of some strong backcourt options. Maybe, after evaluating the opposition for the week, the coach would want stronger corner or stronger inside options. It is a coach's decision, one which the balance of a close game could hinge upon.

We do not intend to present all the quickies we have used in our fourteen years of coaching. That would require more than a chapter. The ones outlined, however, have worked marvelously for us. But thinking coaches can create others. The diagrammed options shown below only serve as excellent examples of the quickie assault.

STRONG BACKCOURT OPTIONS

Diagram 9-1 displays strong scoring opportunities for either guard. 1, while dribbling downfloor, passes inside to 4 who used a screen by 5 to insure himself of being open. 1 dips around 3's blind screen for a pass and a lay up. 3, in compliance with the basketball rules, must set the blind screen at least one step behind X1. 2 meanwhile dips around 4 on a blast maneuver. A handoff to 2 gives him the jump shot. If 2 does not get the ball from 4, he continues around 3 for a pass and either a lay up or a jump shot, depending upon X2's coverage. Should 4 hand off to 2 and X2 or X4 prevent the jump shot, 4 can continue toward 3, aiming to set a double screen. Also this allows 2 to check 1 coming around 5's screen. 2 could operate one-on-one or dribble around 3 for the jumper. If 4 keeps the ball, he checks 1 coming around 5's screen. A perfect route by 1 gets him the jumper as X1 rubs off on 5. If X5 switches a pass to 5 gets the mismatched power lay up.

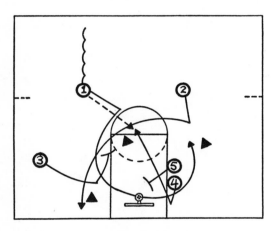

Diagram 9-1

Diagram 9-2 will net 2 an easy high percentage shot. In fact, this quickie has never failed us. 4 again gets a screen from 5, trying to get open as in Diagram 9-1. If 1 does not direct a pass inside to 4, 3 pops out toward the sideline. Upon passing to 3, 1 runs a give and go, stopping a few feet below the free throw line but outside the lane. 4 circles on over to the area of the double screen. 2 meanwhile has dipped to break around the double screen set by 1 and 4. If X3 plays low and toward the basket, attempting to prevent the pass into 2, 3 can drive around the double screen for the jumper. If X3 plays straight, 2 will get the six feet jumper behind the double screen of 4 and 1.

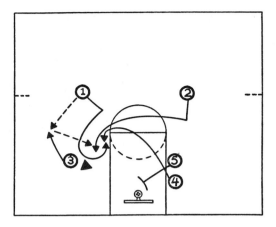

Diagram 9-2

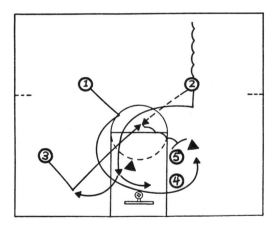

Diagram 9-3

Diagram 9-3 shows the strongside guard dribbling the ball into front court. 3 times his dip, flashing outside the lane only as far as it takes to free himself for a pass. 1 times his backdoor cut to coincide with X1's glance inside toward the pass from 2 to 3. Should X1 not watch the pass from 2 to 3, 1 creates his own backdoor cut by following the techniques described in Chapters 2 and 5. A bounce pass from 3 would get 1 the lay up. If 1 does not get the return pass, 2 dips around 3, running the blast, while 1 continues around the double screen set by 4 and 5. A pass from 3 gets 1 the jump shot. If 3 does not feel that 1 is open, 3 dribbles toward 5, setting a triple screen. 1 breaks around 3 for a hand off pass and a jumper or a driving lay up. 2 has the option of continuing around the double screen or breaking toward the weakside corner. If 2 breaks around the double screen, 3 head-hunts X2 while 1 hits 2 for the wide open jumper. If 2 continues into the weakside corner, 1 and 2 would activate the penetration drill *(Chapter 3)*.

Diagram 9-4 exhibits another quickie with 2, the strongside guard, advancing the ball into the front court. 3 sets a blind pick for 1. A bounce pass from 2 gives 1 the lay up. 1 continues around the double screen should nothing develop out of the blind screen. 2 can hit 1 for the jumper behind the double screen. 2 can keep his dribble alive and use 3 for a screen and roll maneuver. 2 can dribble toward the double screen, setting up the triple screen with 5 and 4. In the latter case, all of the options of Diagram 9-3 become available. Or 3 could clear outside, backdooring X3 as he attempts to help X2 on 2's penetration drive.

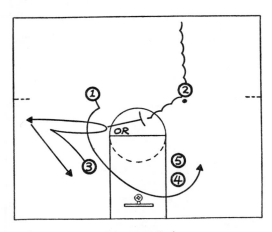

Diagram 9-4

Diagram 9-5 displays a quickie with many options, but the stronger options belong to the backcourt players. 1 passes to 3. 5 flashes across the lane for a pass from 3. To be most effective, the centers need to be good passers. After 5 receives the ball, 1 screens for 2 while 3 begins the splitting series *(Chapters 3, 4, and 5)*. While 2 cuts by 5 on the blast *(Chapter 5)*, 1 continues on his roll around 3 and 4's double screen. If X1 stays in the lane to prevent the lay up, 5 can pass cross-court to 1 who would stay behind 3 and 4 for the jumper. If X1 follows 1 around the double screen, the lay up should result. During these maneuvers, 5 has the center court to work one-on-one.

If a team possesses an outstanding outside shooting big man, Diagram 9-6 will work wonders for the backcourt players and will, most likely, post a big forward on a small guard. 1 passes to 3; and after 5 breaks to the strongside, 1 runs the vertical rub-off *(Chapters 2 and 5)*. 1 continues along the baseline figuring to help screen for 2 who ran a weakside vertical rub-off. Meanwhile 5 pops out for a pass from 3. If X5 did not help on 1's cut, 1 could have the lay up.

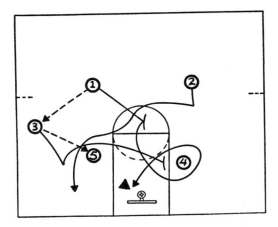

Diagram 9-5

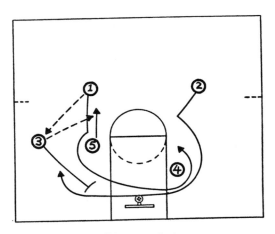

Diagram 9-6

If X5 did help, he cannot possibly get back to cover 5 on the pop out. X5 must honor 5's outside shooting ability by playing him tight. This clears the area where the shots are to occur. 1 should pop around 4's screen for a pass from 5 and a jump shot. If X4 switches, preventing the jumper, then 4 posts X1 inside. A pass from 1 to 4 nets a high percentage shot. Meanwhile 2 has broken around 3's screen, and the same jump shot and posting options take place on the left side of the floor.

After running the Go Behind a few times in succession, X1 gets used to 1 checking 3's posting maneuvers and 1's dribbling around 5's screen and roll *(Diagram 9-7)*. Changing 1's route and 3's responsibility usually nets 1 the lay

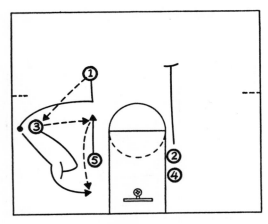

Diagram 9-7

up. 3, instead of continuing around the weakside double screen, sets a strongside pick. 5, instead of screening for 1's dribbling maneuvers, pops out for a pass from 1. As the ball flies toward 5, 1 runs a horizontal rub-off on 3. 3, who is facing the basket, watches X3. If X3 switches onto 1, the only way to prevent the lay up, 3 pops out for a quick jumper.

Or to run the Go Behind's above change up a little bit differently: 3 could hand off to 1 and pop out around 5 (Diagram 9-7). 1 immediately hits 3 while 5 slides down the lane, slightly outside of it. 5 sets a pick facing the basket. 1 runs a horizontal rub-off on 5 who watches X5. X5 must switch onto 1 or concede the lay up. But if X5 switches, 5 pops outside for the jumper.

In either of the last two cases, the play can continue into the Go Behind. These two examples show how one man's duties can be changed ever so slightly resulting in a quickie lay up.

These options by no means complete the passing-dribbling quickies. We run a quickie at the end of every quarter. That means that we must have four ready per game. Sometimes we even get two quickies off at the end of a quarter. For example, we score with five seconds left in a quarter. We press. Our opponents commit a violation. We get a second quickie, but this quickie must come from out of bounds (see section in Chapter 11 on out of bounds). Most of the time we score on our quickies. That is certainly disheartening to our opposition.

STRONG CORNER OPTIONS

Diagram 9-8 depicts the quickest quickie for the cornermen. As 2 dribbles into front court, 3 breaks around the double screen. 3 should get the jump shot. 3 can continue around the double screen for the lob pass near the goal. Another

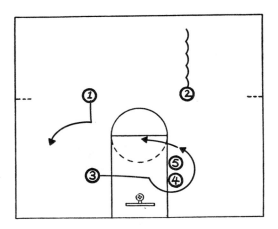

Diagram 9-8

immediate and obvious quickie would be 5's screen down for 4. Or 5 could stand still, letting 4 maneuver X4 into 5. Or 4 could use 5's screen and 3's encirclement as a double screen.

Diagram 9-9 achieves for the cornermen what Diagram 9-5 accomplishes for the backcourt men. 2 receives a pass from 1 and watches 1 set a screen down for 3. If 3 is open for the jumper, 2 hits him. If nothing develops, 3 comes toward 2 while 1 pops outside. As 3 starts over the top of 5, X3 must follow or 2 can pass to 3 for the jump shot. 2 then begins his drive toward center court. As 3 comes around 4 on the low side of the double screen, he should rub X3 off on 4. A pass from 2 gets the lay up. In case 2 dribbles inside the lane and gets in trouble, he can use 1 as a safety valve.

When a team possesses a good jump shooting cornerman, *Diagram 9-10* offers a golden opportunity. 1 passes to 3 and goes behind 3 for the pass back. 3 starts into the area where he would rub his man off on the post man when running the Go Behind *(Chapter 8)*. 3 suddenly dips hard toward 5, only about two feet from him. 2, who had been dipping toward the Go Behind, changes directions, timing his move toward 5 to coincide with 3's. 2, 3, and 5 execute a near perfect triple screen. 4 influences toward the basket before breaking off 5's shoulder. 1 hits 4 for the wide open twelve foot jumper.

STRONG POST OPTIONS

An excellent offensive coach once told the author that the simplest patterns were the most effective. This next option does not quarrel with that observation. 5 times his move to break off 4 as 4 flashes toward the ball. A pass from 1 nets 5 a lay up *(Diagram 9-11)*.

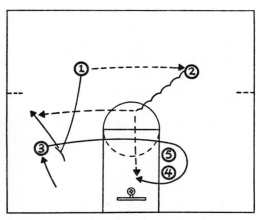

Diagram 9-9

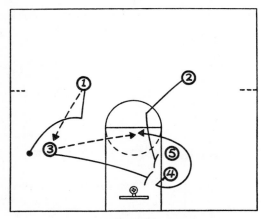

Diagram 9-10

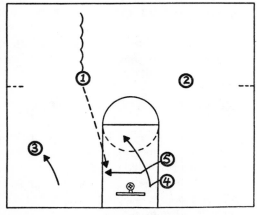

Diagram 9-11

Another way we run this quickie has 4 swing and go around 5, only 4 does not look to receive the ball. Instead 4 completely circles 5. 5 times 4's encirclement to break off 4's back for either the lay up or the jump shot. 5 should break in the direction that would best rub X5 off. That direction, of course, depends upon X5's coverage.

Diagram 9-10 can also be used to award a quickie to a center as well as a cornerman. Instead of 4 breaking around the triple screen, 5 can break around the double screen. Or 5 can break baseline side of 4 which would make use of the triple screen.

A post player who can score over a double screen would welcome the quickie described in *Diagram 9-12*. After 1 passes to 2, he sets the double screen with 3. Meanwhile, 4 has dipped toward the basket and starts up the lane, setting a perfect moving screen on X5. 5 times his move, breaking around 4 at the exact moment when X4 would have to concede a lay up or switch. During this screening, 2 has dribbled toward the middle near the free throw circle. 2 first checks 5 inside; but if it is risky to pass inside, 2 waits for 5 to clear the double screen off 1 and 3.

Although we have used many other quickies, the figures and the reasons given above for using quickies should convince the reader of the wisdom of such offensive change ups. This discussion should also give the coach some ideas of how to create his own quickie system.

QUICKIES AGAINST THE ZONES

Offensive minded coaches agree that screening against zones become less and less effective as the game progresses. Good zone defenders read the screens; and on the second or third running, they are prepared to stop the screening plays. But screens as quickies, run only once or twice a game, cannot be remembered even by the best defender. Nor can the smartest defender defense it.

A book could be written on the zone quickies we have used over the years. But primary intention of this text is to develop a complete free moving offensive system, not just the quickies. A system, we hope, a coach can add to as his material demands. So a few quickie zone examples should suffice.

STRONG BACKCOURT OPTIONS

Our basic zone alignment, after the first passing-dribbling option, is the Overload *(Diagram 9-13)*. After 3 receives the pass and 1 stations himself in the corner, 5, who has crossed the lane looking for the pass inside, rolls to weakside free throw line to set the baseline screen for 1 when the ball is reversed. 4 can set a double screen with 5, or 4 can break outside aiding the reversal of the ball. 1 must be set, ready to shoot, when he receives the pass. Against the 2-3 zone, 5

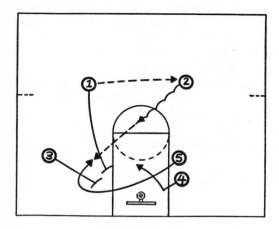

Diagram 9-12

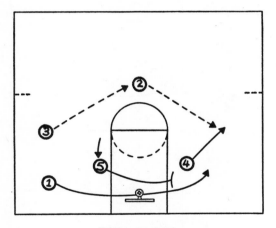

Diagram 9-13

would screen a defensive forward; versus a point zone (1-3-1 and 1-2-2), 5 would screen a baseline defender.

3 could, of course, screen a wing or a guard defender allowing 2 to get the dribbling jump shot. 4 could also screen for 2.

STRONG CORNER OPTIONS

When 3 passes the ball to 2, he breaks through the center. Usually 2 can hit 3 in the middle of the lane. The defensive center covers 5, leaving 3, the flashing high wingman, free. If 3 can get the pass, 3, 1, and 5 can run the penetration drill. Or 3 can jump shoot or pass to 1 for the jumper *(Diagram 9-14)*.

2 can fake a pass back to 1 who filled the area vacated by 3. This fake pass not only draws the defense back to its left, but it gives 5 time to get to the baseline and screen for 3 in the corner.

3 could pass to 1 in the corner instead of reversing the ball to 2. After passing to 1, 3 breaks on low side of 5. 5 follows on a roll to the basket. If 5 does not get the pass, he goes to weakside rebounding area. 1 reverses the ball to 2 who passes to 4. Meanwhile 5 has set a baseline screen, and 3 has prepared himself for a pass and a quick jumper.

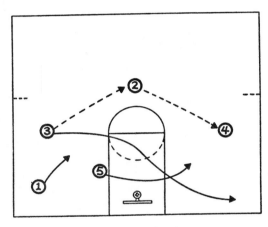

Diagram 9-14

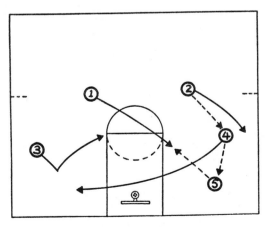

Diagram 9-15

Diagram 9-15 shows our favorite quickie to get 3 the jumper or 4 the lay up. 5 breaks out to the corner to receive the pass from 4. 1 and 2 immediately move toward the ball. Most of the time 5 can bounce pass to 1. 1 can pass to 3 for the jumper, to 4 for the lay up, or to 5 who breaks back toward the goal on the baseline. If 5 cannot get the ball inside to 1, an excellent ball handler, he slaps the ball. The slapping of the ball keys 3, 4, and 1 to rotate their positions clockwise (counterclockwise if 5 is in the opposite corner). Whenever the inside passing lane is blocked on the first slapping, the players roll again. However on the last roll, the positions are filled five to eight feet higher. This not only gives us an area to release the pass to, but it gives us an excellent chance to reverse the ball. This is an excellent quickie against zone teams that overshift to one side of the court.

STRONG POST OPTIONS

An excellent jump shooting center or a big, strong post man would fit well into the quickie described in *Diagram 9-16*. 1 passes to 3 and stands still. This should freeze both the defensive guard and the defensive wing or forward. 2 begins his cut as though he is going to the baseline as in our Overload. Both the defensive center and the baseline defender would see 2's move and anticipate his cut. This should help 4 sneak around the baseline defender for good inside positioning and a pass from 3. Meanwhile 2 has screened the defensive center and 5 has positioned himself for a pass from 3 and a jump shot. If 3 hits 4, 5, who should have the ball side position on the defensive center, breaks in a straight line toward the goal for a pass from 4 and a power lay up.

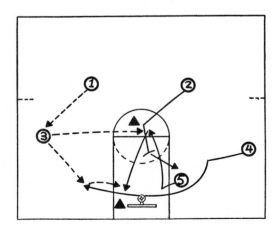

Diagram 9-16

Another power quickie is presented in *Diagran 9-17* which we use only against a 1-3-1 zone. We teach quickies that we use only when anticipating our opponent to run a particular zone. This quickie is presented to show how quickies can be applied to only one type of zone defense. The coach can dream up many others.

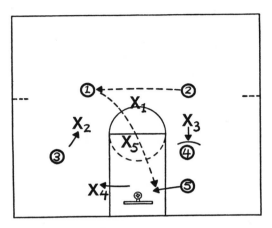

Diagram 9-17

This play is designed to defeat the proper slides of X3 in a conventional 1-3-1 zone. X3 covers 2 when 2 has the ball. 2 passes to 1 while 4 sets a blind screen on X3. A lob pass goalward gets 5 the lay up. Should X4 play the lob pass to 5, 1 can hit 3 for the easy jumper. X5 could sink to cover either 5 or 3. 4, however, could defeat X5's sinking tactic by breaking across the middle. This would give 4 the easy 5 feet jumper. It is impossible for the customary 1-3-1 zone slides to prevent a lay up to this quickie.

CHAPTER 10

The Passing-Dribbling Game: Secrets of The Full Court Game

The full court game, the fast break and the press breakers, are only extensions of the half court game, making the passing-dribbling full court assault a complement to its half court attack. Several two minute periods each game prevent victory or permit it. Alert coaches prepare their teams to excel during those moments when momentum favors them. Going to the full court game creates more possessions, speeds up the contest, allows more scoring. A coach whose teams fast breaks while pressing during intervals of momentum and slows the ball down while playing a drop back defense during times of lag has the best chance of winning. Teams that are not taught fast break tactics lose all runaway games and make close games that they should win going away.

SECRETS OF THE PASSING-DRIBBLING GAME'S FAST BREAK

As in the passing-dribbling half court game, the full court fast break is a free-styling offense. The passing-dribbling free styling fast break however does not permit players to run in a helter-skelter, fire brand fashion but a controlled, systematized order. Players have a freedom of choice based upon sound rules and tried principles, perfected only through hours of drilling. Before explaining the little points of coaching and teaching the passing-dribbling fast break, fundamentals of fast breaking and pressure breaking are taught through the following progressive drills.

The Three Drill Offensively

Procedure (Diagram 10-1)

1. Line all players up in a straight line at the end of the court.

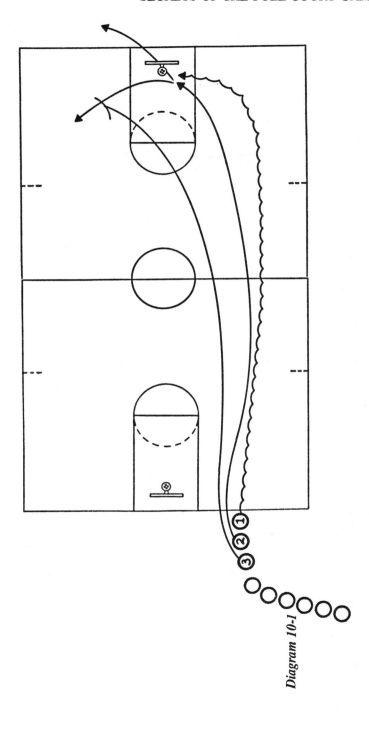

Diagram 10-1

2. The first three players in line activate the three drill: 1 drives the length of the floor for a lay up; 2 lets 1 reach the foul line, fifteen feet away, and then he tries to catch 1 before 1 can drive the remaining seventy-five feet and lay the ball in; 3 races down floor to guard 1 as he tries to receive the throw in.
3. After 1's lay up, 2 takes the ball out of bounds. 3 guards 1 (face guard, denial, sluff or whatever the coach wants) while 2 tries to pass ball in bounds.
4. When ball is inbounded, 1 and 2 fast break while 3 defends.
5. Coach can require 1 and 2 to pass the ball all the way up floor, or 1 and 2 could dribble to half court and pass beyond half court, or 1 and 2 could dribble the length of the court. After learning the entire procedure, coach should let 1 and 2 make their own judgments, correcting any faults at the end of their play.
6. If 3 face guards 1, then 1 must receive the inbounds pass below the free throw line. This situation simulates having a deeper defender to steal any lob pass.
7. The second group of three begins their drill when the first group reaches midcourt on the return trip.

Objectives

1. To condition for the game of basketball: quick starts, quick stops, racing the length of the floor, etc. We do not like to run sprints. Players do not like to run sprints. Besides wasting precious time, which would be devoted to other phases of basketball, running sprints sap the energy and more importantly the enthusiasm of fast break ball players. Conditioning, we contend, should be a by-product of the full court drills. We discovered early in our coaching career that players save energy during practice so that they can run their sprints at the end of practice. This teaches bad habits. Too often three second sprints run at the end of practice take five or six seconds. This not only condones loafing, but it is not as good for building the body system for the game of basketball to lazily jog six seconds instead of sprinting hard three seconds. Give the athlete a ball in a drill and his three second sprints become three seconds. Also sprints at the conclusion of practice, even when followed by a fun drill, leave the players with a bad taste for basketball practice. We like our players to be eager for more at the end of practice, and we want them enthusiastic for the next practice. Full court drilling is the best game conditioner a coach has.
2. To teach 1 to drive hard the length of the floor and to hit the lay up even when he hears footsteps. The lay up is a high jump, not a broad jump. Coaching point: tell the driver that the baseline is the edge of a cliff. To go over the baseline is like jumping off a cliff.

3. To teach 2 to catch 1 and block the shot or foul preventing the easy lay up.
4. To teach 2 to get the pass inbounded against pressure or denial defense, teaching the first phase of attacking a press.
5. To teach 1 to free himself from a denial defender.
6. To teach 3 the proper techniques of face guard pressuring, of denial defense, of sagging.
7. To teach 1 and 2 how to pass while moving at great speeds.
8. To teach 1 and 2 how to attack one defender on a fast break.
9. To teach 3 how to delay the two-on-one fast break until defensive help arrives.
10. All of our full court drills are multi-purpose, teaching many of the offensive and defensive phases of our full court game; and they include such a small number of participants that the coach can easily see and correct mistakes of the players. When ten men are scrimmaging, it is impossible to observe all the activity and inactivity.

The Three Drill Defensively

Procedure (Diagram 10-2)

1. Line players up as in the three drill offensively. It is easy for the players to remember the drills: three drill—three men; offensively (two attackers—one defender), defensively (two defenders—one attacker).
2. 1, 2, and 3 perform the same duties on their trip downfloor as they did in the three drill offensively.
3. After 2 gets the rebound, however, he does not throw the ball into 1 because 1 has become a defender. Instead 2 tries to dribble the length of the court against the repeated double teams of 1 and 3.
4. 1 and 3 try to force 2 to dribble off the court, exiting by the baseline corner.

Objectives

1. To condition.
2. To teach 1 the driving lay up under pressure.
3. To teach 2 to catch 1 before the lay up.
4. To teach 2 to keep his dribble alive, the perfect attack against man-to-man full court pressure, against a run and jump defense, against a team defense that is slow setting up its defense.
5. To teach 1 and 3 proper double teaming techniques, and to teach the two defenders how to control and dominate one attacker.
6. To teach one player how to attack two defenders and either get the good shot or the lay up.
7. To teach two defenders how to stop the one-on-two fast break.

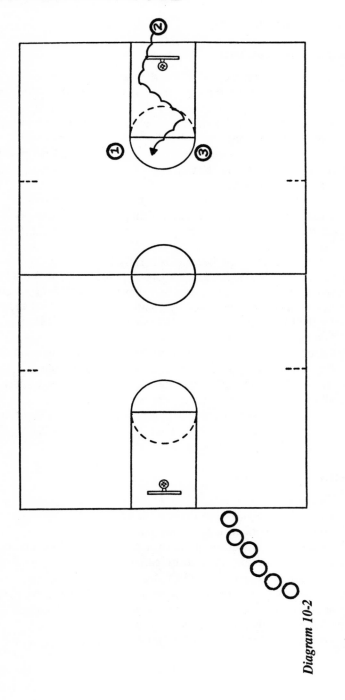

Diagram 10-2

The Four Drill Offensively

Procedure (Diagram 10-3)

1. Line squad up at the end of the floor as in the three drills.
2. 1, 2, and 3 perform the same feats on their trips downfloor as they did in the three drills.
3. 4 races downfloor to touch the baseline. 4 times his return trip to coincide with 2's inbounding the ball to 1.
4. 3 defends (denial, face guard, sag—coach's choice) the pass to 1. 1 must receive the ball below the free throw line extended. 1 must maneuver to get open under pressure.
5. Once the ball is inbounded, it is a three-on-one fast break.
6. 1 can take the center lane with 2 filling the outside lane, or 2 can take the center lane with 1 filling outside. This requires 1 and 2 to make a proper fast break choice.
7. The dribbler, 1 in the diagram, brings the ball down the center lane. 2 and 4 fill the outside lanes, running about three feet inbounds until they reach the free throw line extended, then they make a forty-five degree cut toward the basket. The cut is preceded by planting the outside foot and pushing hard for the basket. 2 and 4 can cross underneath or they can stop at free throw line baseline. We prefer for 2 and 4 to stop.
8. Coach can require players to pass the ball, dribble, or combine the two as they run the length of the floor at full speed. Coach can have attackers weave (dribble) length of the floor or run the figure eight (passing). Use of all of these methods force the attackers to think and to adjust instantly to different fast break situations. Varying the routine will not only teach the players more fast break basketball, but the variety will keep the drill fresh for the duration of the long basketball season.

Objectives

1. To condition.
2. To teach 1 the full court driving lay up.
3. To teach 2 to catch 1 before the lay up.
4. To teach the proper offensive maneuvers for the three-on-one fast break.
5. To teach advancing the ball by passing.
6. To teach advancing the ball by dribbling.
7. To teach a lone defender to slow down the three-on-one break until help arrives, always being cognizant of preventing the lay up.
8. To teach 3 how to defense against inbound passing.
9. To teach 1 to free himself for an inbound pass.

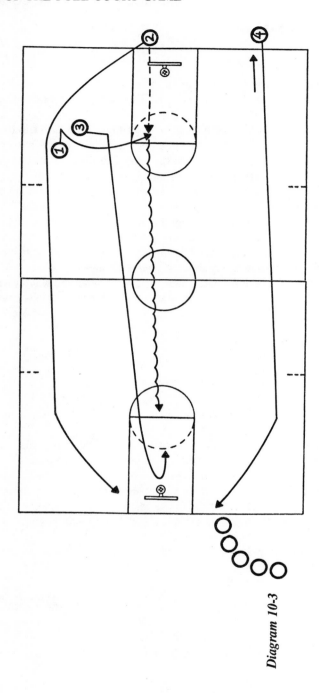

Diagram 10-3

The Four Drill Defensively

Procedure (Diagram 10-4)

1. Line players up at end line as in the other drills.
2. 1, 2, and 3 have the same responsibilities on their trip downfloor as in the other drills.
3. 4, instead of racing to the baseline and timing his return trip to correspond to 2's passing the ball in to 1, defends 2, the inbounds passer. This puts added pressure on 2 to pass successfully inbounds. It also helps drill 2 on inbounding passes against a set full court defense.
4. Once ball is inbounded, 1 and 2 attack 3 and 4 in a two-on-two fast break situation.
5. 3 defends 1 by face guarding, denial, or sluff. 4 tries to keep 2 from spotting 1 or from passing cleanly to him.
6. 3 and 4 can retreat quickly to a tandem defense or they can run and jump, double team, or use any defense coach dictates.
7. 1 and 2 can screen for each other, weave, pass all the way down the floor, dribble all the way down the floor, or combine the two, or whatever the coach prescribes.

Objectives

1. To condition.
2. To teach techniques of a two-on-two fast break.
3. To drill on inbounding passes versus pressure defenses.
4. To teach two skilled athletes to attack pressure defenses from the out of bounds pass to the lay up.
5. To teach two-on-two full court offensive and defensive play.
6. To teach 3 denial, face guarding, or containment defense.
7. To teach 1 to free himself to receive the inbound pass against pressure.
8. To teach 3 and 4 tandem defense, full court man pressure, double teaming, run and jump, and other defensive tactics.
9. To teach proper methods of pressuring the inbound passer.

The Five Drill Offensively

Procedure (Diagram 10-5)

1. Line the squad up at the end of the court as in the other drills.
2. 1, 2, 3, and 4 perform the same functions on their trip down floor as they performed in the four drill offensively.
3. 5 covers 4, trying to prevent the inbounds pass. His defense may be face

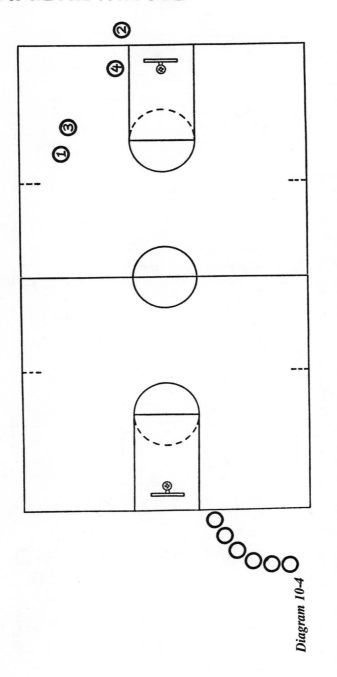

Diagram 10-4

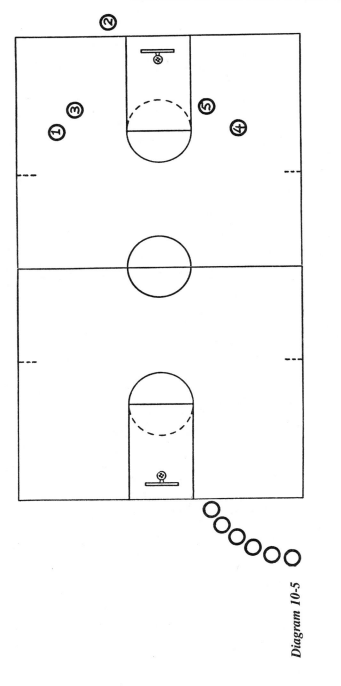

Diagram 10-5

guard, denial, or sluff (coach's choice). If it is a face guard or denial press, 4 must receive the ball below the free throw line extended. This simulates a deep defender intercepting an errant lob pass.

4. In the early stages of the drill, before all concerned become proficient at their skills, 1 and 4 cannot cross against face guard pressure. After 2, 3, and 5 learn the proper offensive and defensive face guarding tactics and become adept at the execution of them, 1 and 4 not only can cross, but they can line in a tandem or any other method of attack they choose or the coach directs. It is good to practice the offensive methods and the methods employed by the opposition.

5. Once 2 passes inbounds to either 1 or 4, they fast break against 3 and 5. Coaches can require the three attackers to pass the ball only, to dribble only, or to combine the two.

6. 3 and 5 can play pressure defense after the ball is passed inbounds, or they can race back to defend in a tandem near their goal.

7. Should 3 or 5 intercept any pass, they fast break against 1, 2, and 4.

8. The guard who receives the inbounds pass should fill the center lane while 2 and the other guard fill the outside lanes.

Objectives

1. To condition.
2. To teach 2 to complete the inbound pass against denial or face guard pressure.
3. To teach 1 and 4 all the different team methods and techniques of eluding denial or face guard pressure.
4. To teach 3 and 5 the tandem or safety defense, so vital to defensing the fast break and as the last line of defense when a press is broken.
5. To teach 1, 2, and 4 how to fast break against two defenders, and to teach them which lane to fill on a three-on-two fast break.
6. To teach 3 and 5 to fast break immediately after stealing an errant pass.
7. To teach 3 and 5 face guarding, denying, or sagging full court defense.
8. To teach passing while moving at full speed.

The Five Drill Defensively

Procedure (Diagram 10-6)

1. Line all players up at the end of the court.
2. 1, 2, and 3 perform the same in their trip down the floor as they did in the five drill offensively. This time, however, 5 helps 3 double team 1, the inbound receiver, and 4 puts pressure on 2, the inbound passer.
3. 1 can break anywhere and use any move to get open.

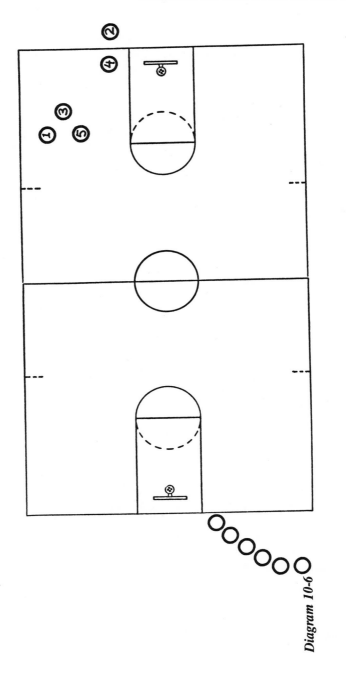

Diagram 10-6

4. 3 and 5 can double team in any manner prescribed by the coach.

5. When the ball is passed inbounds, 3, 4, and 5 run repeated three men run and jumps or recurring double teaming and shooting the gap for interceptions. 1 and 2 attempt a two-on-three fast break.

6. If 3, 4, and 5 intercept, and interceptions should be the rule rather than the exception, they fast break against the two defenders, 1 and 2. This teaches 3, 4, and 5 to fill the lanes on a fast break after making a steal. This drill is an invaluable aid to teaching the fast break off interceptions.

Objectives

1. To condition.
2. To teach 1 to free himself from double teaming tactics so that he can receive the inbounds pass.
3. To teach 2 to make an accurate inbounds pass against great pressure.
4. To teach fast breaking after making an interception.
5. To teach two attackers to fast break against three defenders.
6. To teach 4 to apply pressure on the out of bounds passer.
7. To teach various phases of team defense.
8. To teach dribblers how to avoid the double team and how not to lose their poise or lose the ball when faced with double teaming tactics.

Six Drill Offensively

Procedure (Diagram 10-7)

1. Line up all players except two at the end line as in the five drill defensively. Line up those two in the corners on the opposite end line.

2. 1, 2, 3, 4, and 5 perform the same responsibilities on their trip downfloor as they did in the five drill offensively.

3. 6 races downfloor and assumes a position out of bounds in either the outside lanes or the middle lane. 6 has the choice. Different positioning by 6 aids all players in learning to adjust to the rules of the passing-dribbling fast break (explained next).

4. After the ball is passed inbounds, 2 and 6 must decide on the lanes they are to fill, and the drill becomes a four-on-two fast break. For example: 2 passes into 1 who hits 4 breaking to the middle lane; 6 fills the outside lane vacated by 4 and 2 becomes the trailer (see rules section later in this chapter).

5. If 1, 2, 4, and 6 do not get the immediate lay up or the easy jump shot, they activate the Taint Offense (see a later section in this chapter).

6. 3 and 5 run a tandem defense against the four man assault. Or 3 and 5

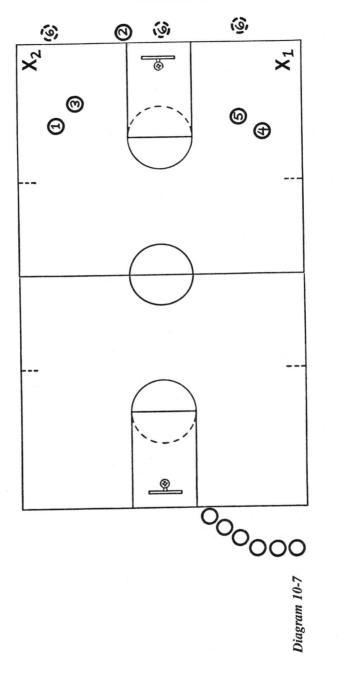

Diagram 10-7

play a parallel defense. 1, 2, 4, and 6 learn to attack both. Coach should use the defense his opposition for the week will use.

7. After 1, 2, 4, and 6 score or 3 and 5 intercept, the two defenders, 3 and 5, along with the trailer (changes each trip) attack X1 and X2 in a three-on-two trip downfloor.

8. When X1 and X2 stop this three men assault or when the three attackers score, X1 and X2 attack the middle lane man, which will change with each trip, in a two-on-one fast break situation.

9. The two outside men in the three-on-two fast break stay downfloor becoming the new X1 and X2.

10. A new six begin another wave of action as the two-on-one fast break reaches midcourt.

Objectives

1. To condition.

2. To teach the four-on-two, the three-on-two, and the two-on-one fast break situations.

3. To force players to adjust constantly when recovering a loose ball or a rebound by immediately racing to their lanes for the fast break.

4. To teach the never ending, non-repeating, fast paced action of a basketball game in a controlled scrimmage with the number of players small enough for the coach to follow and correct.

5. To teach 3 and 5 pressure defenses and how to retreat into a tanden or parallel fast break defense.

6. To teach 2 and 6 to adjust to the proper lane, following the rules of the passing-dribbling game's fast break, explained later in this chapter.

7. To teach proper defense of the four-on-two, the three-on-two, and the two-on-one situations.

The Six Drill Defensively

Procedure (Diagram 10-8)

1. Line the squad up at the end of the court like in the three, four, and five drills.

2. 1, 2, 3, 4, and 5 perform the same duties as in the five drill offensively.

3. 6 puts pressure on 2, the inbounds passer. Or 6 can drop back to free throw line to intercept any errant lob pass. The coach decides which and his decision should be based upon the type of press his next opponent employs.

4. 3, 5, and 6 can run any type press the coach wants: straight man-to-man, give the outside, then take it away, force the reverse dribble and double team, run and jumps of all types, double teaming and shooting the gap with an interceptor.

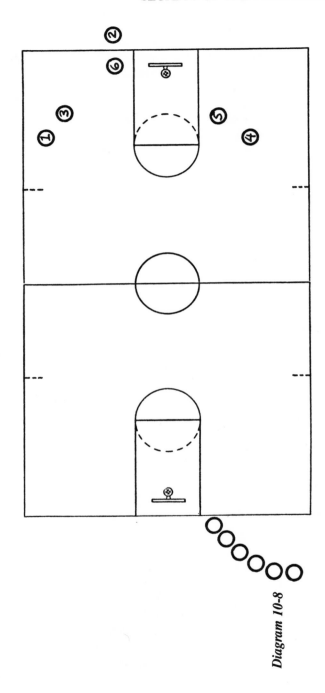

Diagram 10-8

5. 1, 2, and 4 must become expert ball handlers to defeat the different double teams and pressures.
6. 1, 2, and 4 will fast break, if possible, against the three defenders 3, 5, and 6.
7. If no fast break is available, 1, 2, and 4 can go directly into our Taint Offense.
8. If 3, 5, and 6 can intercept any pass, they will fast break against 1, 2, and 4. And the same six begin the drill again.

Objectives

1. To condition.
2. To teach 1, 2, and 4 how to break a press.
3. To teach 1, 2, and 4 how to fast break against three opponents.
4. To teach 1 and 4 to defeat face guard and denial pressure.
5. To teach 2 how to prevent the five seconds violation and yet not throw the ball away or lose his poise.
6. To teach 3, 5, and 6 our full court defensive system.
7. To teach 1, 2, and 4 our Taint Offense (see later section in this chapter).
8. To teach 3, 5, and 6 how to press yet get down floor on defense in time to play a tandem or a triangular defense and deny any lay up.
9. To teach 3, 5, and 6 how to fast break should they intercept a pass.

The 3, 4, 5 , and 6 drills teach the fundamentals that we will discuss in the sections on fast break rules and on the rules of breaking the press. After proper work on these fundamentals, the same drills can be used to prepare a team both offensively and defensively for the next opponent. The coach should choose his drills to comply with the techniques his opponents will employ and how he intends to defeat those techniques.

The 3, 4, 5, and 6 drills teach the fast break after the outlet pass. But as all coaches know, the outlet pass makes the fast break. And although we initially teach the outlet passing techniques with break down drills, the drill below consolidates all the essentials of getting the break started. Once started, the 3, 4, 5, and 6 drills will keep it going until it culminates in the easy high percentage shot. How the break starts ultimately determines the speed and the effectiveness of the break.

The Outlet Pass Fast Break Drill

Procedure (Diagram 10-9)

1. Divide squad into three lines.
2. First man in each line is a defensive rebounder.
3. Second man in each line is an offensive rebounder.

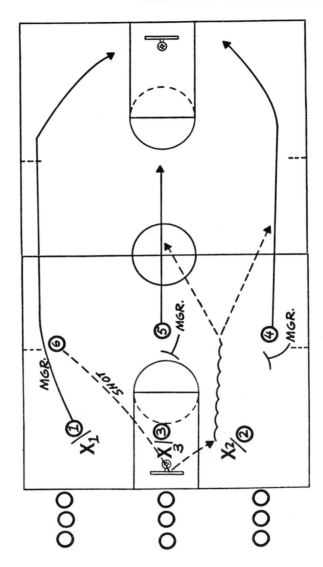

Diagram 10-9

4. Third man in each line passes the ball around with the third man in the other two lines until one of them shoots. Then the third man becomes the outlet pass receiver.

5. Should X1, X2, or X3 play poor defense, 4, 5, or 6 may pass inside for the easy shot.

6. The managers can step in front of the third man (4, 5, or 6) anytime after a shot has been taken. They don't step in front on every shot, but they should about two times out of three.

7. For discussion sake, we will let the rebound carom off to X2. X1 and X3 must also box out. When X2 secures the rebound, X1 releases to fill the left outside lane. X2 checks outside outlet receiver on his side of the court. If manager is fronting 4, then 4 releases on a fly. If the manager stayed out of the play, X2 hits 4 with the outlet pass. Meanwhile the manager on 5 must decide to front or not. If 4 is fronted, X2 checks 5. If 5 is not fronted, X2 throws the outlet pass to 5. If 5 is also fronted, X2 blasts out, takes a long dribble, and passes to either 4 or 5, both of whom have begun their race down the floor in accordance with the passing-dribbling game fast break rules.

8. The rebounder pivots on the foot nearest the sideline. If he is unable to find the outlet pass receiver immediately, he glances toward the middle court area. If the secondary receiver is not open, then he continues his pivot into an explosive blast, followed by a long dribble before beginning his short dribbles or passing downfloor.

Objectives

1. To teach X2 to check the outlet pass areas after securing the rebound but before he hits the floor.
2. To teach the blasting dribble technique.
3. To teach proper defensive blockouts.
4. To teach offensive rebounding.
5. To teach filling the lanes on the fast break.
6. To teach outlet passing techniques.

The coach can place two defenders in a tandem on the other end of the floor. Then the three attackers can run a three-on-two fast break. The coach could add a fourth attacker, creating a four-on-two break. Another defender could be added, permitting the triangular defense to be run. The outlet pass fast break drill possesses versatility.

As a rule the point defender and outlet pass receiver runs the fly when he is covered defensively. This usually opens the court for a better outlet pass to the secondary outlet pass receiver. And teams that look to steal the outlet pass are vulnerable at their defensive end of the court.

If we can force the defensive guards to retreat and to play defense on our offensive end and if their three big men hit their offensive boards, then there is a distance of forty to fifty feet where there are no defenders. In other words, there is a seam in the first line of retreat (guards) and the second line of departure (the offensive rebounders). This first line creates the tandem or parallel defense or they try to intercept the outlet pass. The second line either hit the offensive boards hard and fallback slowly or they concede the defensive rebound and race downfloor more swiftly. Either way an advantage is gained by the threat of the break or by the actual break. The outlet pass receivers, unless the primary receiver has gone on a fly, should place themselves in the seam between these two lines for the outlet pass. And away we go.

Fast break teams must come off the defensive boards running. They must use speed in the backcourt and poise and thinking in the front court. We advocate never taking a bad shot off of the break, and we never want to worry about numbers. An uncontested three-on-five or even a one-on-five shot from ten feet is as high a percentage shot as an uncontested three-on-two shot from the same spot. We just do not have as good a chance for the offensive rebound if we miss. But with modern shooters, that shot will be successful seventy percent of the time. And the uncontested ten feet shot one-on-five is better percentagewise than the contested ten feet shot five-on-five.

If the break is not present, we run the Taint Offense from where the players end up off the break. And if we cannot get results from the Taint Offense, we go immediately to the set offense—again from where the players end up. One of the beauties of the passing-dribbling game is its ability to set up immediately, wasting no time to reset, giving the defense no lull time to regroup.

RULES AND THEORIES GOVERNING THE PASSING-DRIBBLING GAME'S FAST BREAK

Nathan Bedford Forrest gained fame during the Civil War with his tactic of "getting there firstus with the mostus." That is and should be the major objective of all fast break plans.

The problem is how does one get there firstus with the mostus. Geometry teaches us that the shortest distance between two points is a straight line. Reason tells us that with speed being equal the man who runs in a straight line arrives first. Hence the first rule, the outlet pass and lane rule: when the defense gains control of the ball, players race in the lane they are in to the other free throw line, then they make adjustments.

The extra lane filler, if there is one, and the outlet pass receiver sometimes operate as exceptions to the first rule. The extra lane filler is comparable to 2 and 6 in the six drill offensively. While on defense, the defender furthest away from the basket in each lane fills that lane. But, often three men are caught near the basket in defensive rebounding position. One of these men is the extra lane filler. He races down the center lane until he reaches midcourt; then he fills the vacant lane, giving the offense scorers in all three lanes. Only he can make that decision, and it must be made quickly at top speed. It will always be the third player crossing the midcourt line.

The other exception to the first rule is the outlet pass receiver. We permit the outlet pass receiver to choose three options, and we prefer for him to vary his choices. He may, upon team recovery of the basketball, immediately fly to his offensive end of the court. This would require for at least one defender to go with him or we get there firstus with the mostus. This also clears an area for the second outlet pass receiver. Now the second decision: cut across the middle for a pass or cut to the outside lane. This decision is based upon where the ball is rebounded. If the outlet pass receiver is in the lane on the side of the rebound, he cuts to the outside. If he is in the far lane and the rebound is secured in the opposite outside lane, he cuts to the middle lane. If the rebounder can hit this outlet pass man, the worst the offense has is a two-on-two break. If unable to hit either of the outlet pass receivers, the rebounder blasts out with a swinging dribble while the outlet pass receivers race downfloor in their lanes in a straight line.

We play man-to-man defense; consequently, it is difficult to assign one man or one position a specific responsibility because they may be too far out of that position when the shot is taken to assume that duty. Zone coaches may use the passing-dribbling game's fast break by assigning both positions and duties. However, we stay in our lanes *(Diagram 10-10)*, and let the players think fast break possibilities. The most important part of the fast break is getting the ball out and the players in a straight line with hard, quick, and fast motion.

Let's say that the shot is taken while the five defenders are in the positions described in Diagram 10-10. X2, an outlet pass receiver chooses between fly, being the point defender, or coming to the left outside lane, which in this case is the rebounding lane. X1 must break toward the rebound lane. X4 can hit X2 on the fly in his lane, or hit X1 across the middle, or can blast out with a swinging dribble. X3 races downfloor in his lane and X5 runs the straight line in his lane. Of course, X4 could hit X1 who could hit X2 or any of the other hundred or so free style options that are available.

The adjustment or second rule occurs after the ball is in motion, near the offensive free throw line. It is here that the decision of which lane to fill must finally be made. We want all three lanes filled, and we want the fourth player downfloor in on the secondary wave of the fast break. And we want these four players involved in the Taint Offense.

Outlet pass receivers fill two lanes. The third player that crosses the midcourt line should veer to the open lane. He should easily recognize which lane is vacant for his two teammates are in front of him. The fourth player that crosses the midcourt line should read the middle player's action. If the middle player

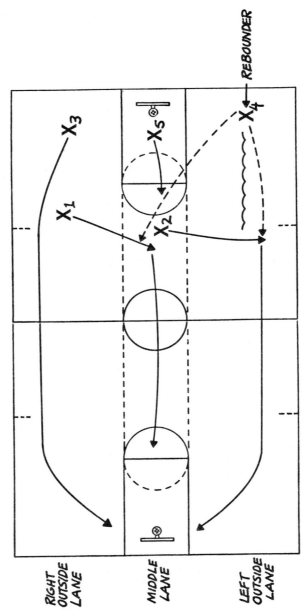

RIGHT
OUTSIDE
LANE

MIDDLE
LANE

LEFT
OUTSIDE
LANE

Diagram 10-10

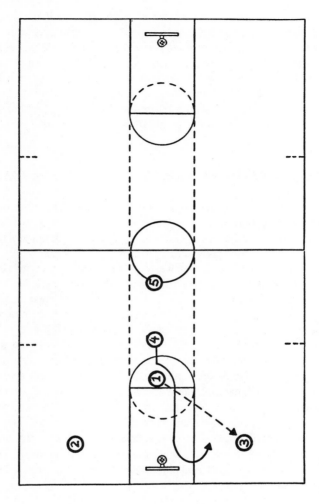

Diagram 10-11

passes to a side and breaks goalward for a return pass, or if the middle player dribbles goalward forcing the defense to react, the fourth player stops at the free throw line for a reverse pass that would defeat a tandem defense. If the middle player passes to a side and stays at the free throw line, the fourth player uses the middle player as a screener as he breaks around the middle player toward the ball on a cut to the low post. The fifth player, although he races hard to the midcourt line, remains as safety near midcourt *(Diagram 10-11)*. In Diagram 10-11, if 3 cannot pass quickly to 4, he might be able to hit him at a stationary low post.

SECRETS OF ATTACKING PARALLEL OR TANDEM DEFENSES

Most teams hit the offensive boards with three men. The other two defenders race downfloor to play fast break defense, hoping to delay a fast breaking team until the offensive rebounders can retreat. These two defenders must either be in a tandem or a parallel defense.

If faced with a parallel defense, we want the middle player to penetrate all the way to the basket or until one of the parallel defenders pick him up. This is the penetration drill described in detail in Chapter 3. If the two defenders play tandem, as most coaches teach, we want the screen and roll or the give and go run. We want these two maneuvers run after the point man has passed to a wing. In other words we want the offense begun from a wing. Point men who do not pass the ball soon finds he has no wing man to pass to. So we require point men to let the wing men receive at least one pass before beginning the screen and roll or the give and go. If it is parallel, the worst we get is the jump shot by the trailer, 4. If it is tandem, the worst is a jumper by 1 or 3, the two outside wing men.

Some teams send only two players to the offensive boards, leaving three defenders to retreat on defense. These three defenders play a triangular fast break defense: a point man and two on the big blocks along the free throw lane. Either the screen and roll or the give and go should net a good shot with excellent rebounding position.

Our fast break wing players are not permitted to continue running out of bounds. They know they will receive a pass because the point player is required to pass to a wing to begin our offense. Continuing out of bounds would take the wing men out of the Taint Offense and would ruin our set patterned or passing-dribbling attack. Going on out of bounds is a fundamental tactical mistake which must not be tolerated.

SECRETS OF THE TAINT OFFENSE

Should the initial wave (the three lane) or the secondary phase (the fourth player) not net a score, we move to the Taint Offense. It Taint fast break, and it Taint set offense; it's just Taint.

The Taint Offense has two basic patterns: the screens and the cuts. To get into the screens, from Diagram 10-11, 3 could pass to 1 and go screen for 1. A tandem or parallel defense could not stop the screened jumper or the roll or a pass to 4 breaking to the corner or 2 moving to the open hole of the tandem zone. Or 3 could pass to 1 who passed to 2, and 3 could run a horizontal rub-off on 4. When three defenders have retreated, 1 could pass to 2, and 4 would still break on 3's side of 1. 2 reverses the ball to 1 who immediately hits 3 who shoots behind 4's screen. All the two and three men options explained in Chapters 1 and 5 are available in the Taint Offense. There are many other screening possibilities which players will instinctively perform after teaching Chapter 5 if screening is encouraged and emphasized by the coach.

Another phase is the cuts, the give and go. Usually this is keyed by 1 passing and going. When 1 passes and cuts, 4 fills in the area vacated by 1. If 1 does not receive a pass back from 3, he moves to the corner strongside. 3 could either pass to 1 and go or pass to 4 and go. Or 4 and 2 could exchange, creating still more difficulty for the tandem or parallel defenses. But whenever a passer gives and goes, the passer must always break on the ball side of his defender. This enables the new receiver to pass the ball back to the give and go cutter.

Whether to run the give and go or the screen and roll sometimes give fast break athletes trouble. Our players use a simple judgment criterion to help them pick their best choice. And the test helps us to place responsibility on a definite athlete's shoulder. The player with the ball must decide before passing the ball if he can break between his defender and the ball. If his judgment is positive, he runs the give and go; if his decision is negative, he runs the screen and roll.

THE 12 DRILL

Our complete offensive and defensive system is taught by drills. The fast break attack is no exception. The earlier drills in this chapter teach the players the fundamentals of the entire full court game (the fast break and the offenses against the press). Now we draw all these fundamentals, thoughts, and theories into a team drill. We believe in controlling scrimmages, and the 12 drill adheres to this. We believe that players learn only by doing, and the 12 drill conforms to that. After mastering the fundamental drills and the 12 drill, the passing-dribbling team can fast break any opponent. And the players, guided by the coach, will be doing the thinking, developing into a championship caliber team.

Procedure (Diagram 10-12)

1. Place four members of the squad at each end of the floor. Let one group wear one color jersey and the other group wear another color. Let the third group begin the drill at midcourt. The third group can wear a third color or no shirt at all. If a coach carries more than twelve squad members, he can provide some fundamental drill for the remainder of the team.

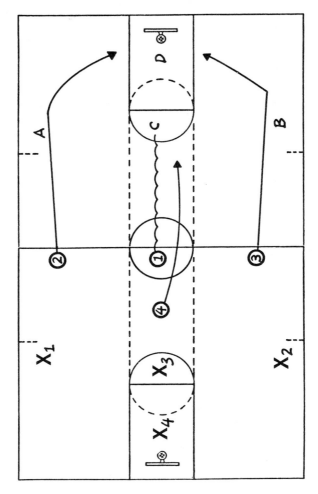

Diagram 10-12

2. 1, 2, 3, and 4 attack C and D, who may defend in a tandem or a parallel defense. It can be altered, or it can represent the next opponent's defense. At times a coach can permit three defenders to form the triangular fast break defense. When the fast breaking team faces the triangular defense, the secondary (trailer) phase must be activated. From the trailer plays, the fast break advances into the Taint Offense.
3. 1, 2, 3, and 4 use all the techniques of our fast break and our Taint Offense.
4. Once C and D rebound the ball or 1, 2, 3, and 4 score, they make an outlet pass to A or B.
5. C and D fill the lanes as A, B, C, and D fast break against X3 and X4.
6. Once X3 and X4 secure the ball, they pass to X1 or X2.
7. Now X1, X2, X3 and X4 attack two of 1, 2, 3, or 4.
8. The groups continue for the prescribed time allocated by the coach, usually four minutes.

Objectives

1. To condition.
2. To teach all the phases of our fast break.
3. To teach the Taint Offense.
4. To teach tandem, parallel, and triangular fast break defenses.
5. To teach thinking and adjusting while moving at full speed, ingredients present in all championship fast break teams.

SECRETS TO BREAKING THE PRESS

Breaking presses, using the free-styling passing-dribbling game, requires, for the most part, short, quick, snappy passes. Against certain pressing defenses the dribble provides the better avenue of attack. So we again teach rules for the players to apply when facing a press. We also have a full court passing game drill which we use to teach passing while moving at top speed as well as the basic fundamentals of breaking a press.

The Full Court Passing Game Drill

Procedure (Diagram 10-13)

1. Line up the squad in groups of five.
2. A team goes down and back twice before another five takes the floor.
3. Run the drill as quickly as possible; 3 to 4 seconds per trip is normal.
4. If 1 passes to 3, 4 breaks toward the ball, receiving the pass from 3. This is the proper fundamental of stepping toward a pass. It is also the area where most press offenses attempt to get the ball.

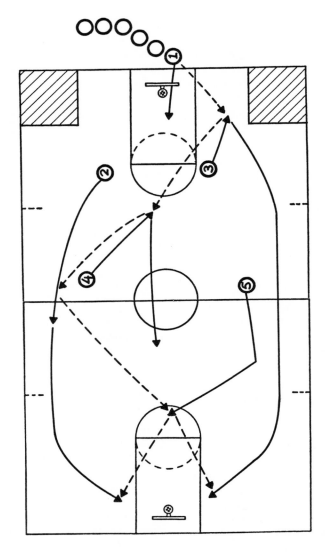

Diagram 10-13

5. 4 immediately pivots and passes to 2 breaking up the outside. 4 reverse pivots on his outside foot. This enables him to protect the ball longer, and it gives him a better peripheral view of 2's cut up the floor.

6. Meanwhile 5 has reversed directions, receiving a pass from 2 about the head of the circle.

7. 5 now has many options. He can pass to either 2 or 3 for the lay up. He can activate any phase of the fast break, including the Taint Offense. Or he can continue the full court passing game drill by hitting either 2 or 3 for the lay up.

8. 4 breaks down the center lane becoming the fourth man in the fast break attack.

9. 2 and 3 exchange sides on the lay up. 1 rebounds the ball out of the basket, which means he really has to sprint the length of the court. 4 and 5 scramble back to their spots. We like to run this drill down and back —down and back—in fifteen seconds or less without ever letting the ball touch the floor.

10. 2 and 3 can line in a tandem and break to a spot. 4 can join the tandem, especially when we face a face guard press.

11. When 1 throws the inbound pass, he steps underneath his defensive basket. This is a safety value passing area, and it is excellent defensive positioning should our opposition intercept a pass.

12. Instead of hitting 4, 3 could hit 5. In that case 4 takes the center lane and 2 the other outside lane. 3 becomes the fourth attacker.

13. If 3 uses the safety value pass to 1, 2 buttonhooks back down the floor, 4 breaks to the midcourt sideline, and 5 posts in the middle area. 3 races in a straight line down his sideline. And the offense continues down the other side of the court.

14. Of course, 3 could pass to 2 on the long fly route.

15. We try never to pass inbounds in the shaded area.

Objectives

1. To condition.
2. To teach the team to get the ball inbounds, to use short, snappy passes, and to post in the center of the floor against all full court presses.
3. To teach different passes while moving at top speed.
4. To teach the fast break offense, the Taint Offense, and the press breaking offense.

RULES OF THE PRESS BREAKER

Before attacking any press, the offensive coach and/or the team must recognize the defensive pressing tactics. If faced with any form of man-to-man, including the run and jumps, keeping the dribble alive will usually suffice to break the defense. If the defense is a straight man-to-man, a clearout by everyone except the best dribbler should be used. The dribbler should reverse his dribble in a looping manner when faced by a run and jump defense.

So the hardest thing about breaking the straight man-to-man press would be the inbound pass. Lining 2, 3, and 4 in tandem should be practiced. Let's say that 2 is in front of 3 who is in front of 4. 3 taps 2 on the side he wants 2 to break. 3 breaks in the other direction, or 3 screens for 4 to break opposite 2's direction. As the ball is inbounded, the others clearout. If it is run and jump, the attacker whose defender is running to activate the run and jump returns downfloor for the outlet pass in case the defense successfully double teams. However, if the dribbler keeps his dribble alive by a looping reverse, breaking the run and jump should be no problem.

Zone presses have become more prevalent since John Wooden's fantastic success with it. Breaking the zone presses requires more team work than breaking a man-to-man press. Usually it is the initial phase of the defense that achieves the most success, especially at the high school level, unless defensive teams have been drilled sufficiently in proper regrouping methods as the ball is advanced down the floor. It is this initial phase and regrouping tactics that our press breaker drill proposes to attack, enabling us to get the lay up at the far end of the court.

Let's again let 2, 3, and 4 *(Diagram 10-13)* line up in a tandem or a parallel attack along the free throw line. It can be arranged by signals which player would break in which direction, using variety in the breaking pattern. Should the initial break not enable the pass to be thrown inbounds, the passing-dribbling game's rule would require for all cutters to move from one lane to another, screening and rolling for each other. For discussion's sake, 3 again breaks to his right, 2 to his left, and 4 down the middle. There are only two zone presses: odd fronts and even fronts. If the press is 1-2-1-1, 3-1-1, 3-2, or 1-2-2, then X1 would have the point, X2 would cover 3 as these attackers move to the corners, leaving 4 open in the middle. A pass out to either 2 or 3 as they break down the sides destroys the zone press. But if X2 and X3 stay tight, preventing the pass into the center lane, a pass to 2 or 3 permits a quick advance of the ball by dribbling up the sideline until X4 cuts him off. The other defenders will race to get ahead of the ball. As X4 and a teammate, depends upon who has been designated as the double-teamer in that particular press, double team the dribbler, he still has the options that were explained in the press breaking drill (Diagram 10-13). The only difference: the offense now has advanced the ball near midcourt.

The only other possible odd zone front is to take a defender off the out of bounds passer and line him up at the free throw line with the other two defenders. This gives the inbounds passer a chance to throw the uncontested baseball pass. So 5 is sent deep, keeping the two deep defenders in the 3-2 or the one deep defender in the 3-1-1 busy. Now the offense floods one side of the court, such as 3 moves near the shaded area, 4 breaks to midcourt area on the same side and in the same lane, and 2 breaks to the midcourt area in the opposite outside lane. 3 now becomes the safety value for 1 if he cannot hit either 2 or 4. Of course the coach can alter the responsibilities and duties of 2, 3, and 4, forcing the defense to keep guessing the routes of 2, 3, and 4. Once the ball is inbounded, if we have the immediate break we take it; if not, we can advance the ball according to the full court passing game drill.

Even zone presses are easier to break because there is no pressure placed on the out of bounds passer. They are of only two types: 2-1-2 or 2-2-1.

If the 2-2-1 zone press is employed, 2 breaks to one outside lane, 3 breaks to the other, and 4 stays in the middle. It is impossible for two men to cover all three passing lanes. A pass to the outside lane means they were not covered and a dribbler can advance the ball to the midcourt area before the second line of defense can stop him. A pass to the inside man means both front line defenders have covered the outside lanes. The inside man pivots and either drives directly up the floor, breaking the press, or passes off to 2 or 3 breaking up the sidelines.

If the 2-1-2 zone press is employed, 5 is sent deep, forcing one of the deep men to cover deep. Remember it is easy to throw a baseball pass with no defender on 1. That leaves the defense in a 2-1-1-1 alignment. We flood the sidelane whose defender followed 5. For example, both 3 and 4 would break to the right sideline (Diagram 10-13), 3 near the shaded area and 4 near midcourt. Then 2 would keep the other deep defender busy by breaking midcourt on the left sideline. 3 again becomes the safety value. Any immediate break we take. Any inbounded pass can be followed by the full court passing game drill. The important thing is to get the ball inbounds and begin a team attack, advancing the ball hurriedly but with poise downcourt. A few lay ups should discourage the press. If it does not discourage the defenders, this attack should result in more than a few lay ups.

CHAPTER 11

The Passing-Dribbling Game: Secrets of Attacking Special Situations

Complete offensive systems provide ways of attacking special situations. When those methods complement the regular or auxiliary offense, it makes them easier to teach, easier to learn, and much more effective.

SECRETS TO BREAKING THE HALF COURT ZONE PRESSES

Half court zone presses consist of two types: the odd and the even fronts. Even zone fronts are not nearly as prevalent as the odd ones. Both types plan to force speedier offensive play, to push the offense farther away from the basket, to keep double team pressure on the good ball handler and/or shooter, and to steal the ball or to stop the stall late in the game. Offenses not only have to be successful against both the odd and even fronts, but they must be able to control and dominate the above purposes of the half court zone press.

With this in mind let's first attack the even front half court zone presses. Even front presses include only the 2-1-2 and the 2-3 alignments. The strengths of both presses lie in the middle. So attacking the even zone presses should be confined to the sidelines. We like to align our men in the holes of the zone presses and run our inside roll. We like to attack in waves, preventing the long pass interception yet looking for the quick immediate score. So against the even half court press we run 13 or 12.

Diagram 11-1 displays the 2-3 half court zone press and our 12 formation. 1 tries to stay out of the trap of X1 and X2. If X1 and X2 want to trap, 1 must force X2 to come far away from his normal defensive area. 2 can stay near the midcourt line for a pass from 1, he can break in front of X5 for a pass and a dribbling penetration, or he can break behind X4 to the baseline for a pass and a lay up. If 1 passes to 3, 1 breaks to middle area of the court and 3 has the option

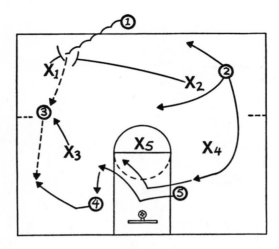

Diagram 11-1

of passing to 5 or 4. When 5 receives a pass inside, 2, if he broke in front of X5, now cuts down the lane to the baseline weakside. If 5 receives the ball, he can pass to 2 or 4 for the lay up. When 3 passes to 4, 5 breaks to the low post and 2 rolls to the high post. If 4 can get the immediate shot or drive, he takes it. If not, he hits 5 low. If none of these options become available, 4 passes to 2 at high post. 5 rolls to opposite side and 4 breaks baseline. 2 can pass to 4 or to 5 for the lay up. If 2 cannot complete one of these options, a pass back outside to 1 can begin the roll again. 1 hits 5 as he moves outside and 4 and 2 begin the inside roll.

Against the odd zone presses, the 1-2-2 or 1-3-1, we line up in a 2-1-2 formation, called 23. Wingmen start high, preventing the long lob pass interception *(Diagram 11-2)*. 1 brings the ball down center of the floor, veering to one side or to the other as he approaches midcourt. His choice depends upon the positioning of X2 and X3. 1 maneuvers to force both defenders to stay high. As X2 comes to midcourt to double team, 1 passes to 3. X4 will not gamble for an interception that high. 5 immediately moves to low post as 4 flashes strongside high. 3 dribble drives toward the baseline. The inside roll becomes operational and all the options available against the even zones are now present versus the odd ones.

If the game is late and we are stalling, we still provide the same attack, only we keep the ball moving, always looking only for the lay up. Occasionally we maintain 5 at a high post and let 4 break to the strongside free throw lane baseline. A pass to 4 at that position keys 5 to move straight down the lane. A pass from 4 to 5 gets 5 the easy lay up.

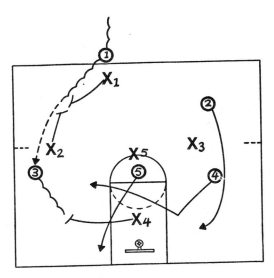

Diagram 11-2

SECRETS OF THE DELAY GAME

The delay game contains two parts: the stall and the deep freeze. The stall, in our vernacular, can be run anytime during the game. It is designed to slow the game down, always looking for the very high percentage shot. The deep freeze is used to protect a lead late in the game, and it is designed for the lay up or a free throw.

We stall to maintain a lead late in a game, to score the last basket at the end of every quarter, to draw the opposition out of a zone into one-on-one play, to protect a player who is in foul trouble, or to gain a strategical advantage. Stalling must be drilled upon and drilled upon to be extremely successful. Because we want the last shot of each quarter, we stall at a minimum of four times each game. So we insist upon perfected execution through repeated drilling.

When we are stalling or freezing the ball, we do not want the dribble used unless it is absolutely necessary. We want the four players away from the ball to have constant motion but never going near the ball handler. When the passer finally must pass the ball, we want the throw to be a hard, two-handed chest pass aimed at a target, which is a hand signal given by the receiver. We want extreme care used in avoiding an offensive foul. We do not want screening either on or away from the ball. The post man is used as an outlet pass receiver whenever the dribbler loses his dribble and is unable to pass to a cornerman or another guard. We want the ball kept out of the corners.

Three attacks comprise the stall and the freeze. Against the man-to-man defense the alignment is always 3-2. Against the zones the original alignment places men in the holes, and we run the inside roll (see section on attacking the half court zone press).

Diagram 11-3 exhibits the original formation against man-to-man. 1 should be an excellent ball handler and a great free throw shooter. 1's three moves are the give and go, the pass and go away from the ball, and the four corners.

1 passes to 3 and breaks down the center of the floor. Should X1 and X3 double team 3, a pass back to 1 gets the three-on-two attack. 1 moves to a high wing giving 3 a large outside area of the court to kill time or penetrate.

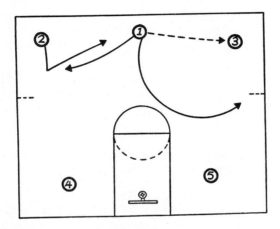

Diagram 11-3

1 can pass to 3 and go away from the ball. A pass back to 2 brings his maneuverability into play. 2 may penetrate or pass to 1 or 3.

The four corner option, originated by Dean Smith, is the best and most used stalling technique in basketball. 1 maneuvers his man by a dribble, looking to penetrate. As he comes down the lane, X4 or X5 must pick him up. A simple lay off pass, preferably a bounce pass, gets the lay up. Of course, 1 can pass to 3 and move to the high wing position, giving 3 the responsibilities of 1.

Basketball rules can force the action below the twenty-eight feet mark. The ball must be advanced below the twenty-eight feet mark every five seconds after the attacking team has been warned by the officials. Every four plus seconds the ball must be dribbled when closely (within six feet) guarded. And every four plus seconds the dribble must be stopped. Each stalling player, therefore, should have a keen sense of time. And each stalling player must be unselfish.

There are also lack of sufficient action rules which the coach must make the individual stallers aware of. This rule makes it mandatory to gain a lead on the openning tip. The team behind must force the action. So if the offense has the lead, the defense is forced to spread itself. If the offense is behind, they must advance the ball beyond the twenty-eight feet line every ten seconds as a team.

Any violation is a technical foul after a team has been warned. In case of a tie, the burden for action lies with the defense.

Most of the time, however, when a team is stalling for the last shot in any quarter, the officials do not warn the offending team. And we like to go for the last shot in all quarters. We do this by either running a quickie *(see Chapter 9)* or by breaking 5 high. We hit 5 and let him drive quickly for the basket. If X4 helps, 4 gets the jumper or the lay up. We do not hit 5 unless the three outside men are covered tightly. And after hitting 5, we want 2 and/or 3 backdooring goalward. If only a few seconds remain, we want 1 also racing toward the goal. Any missed shot should have five offensive rebounders. There is no need for floor balance because the defense will not have time to drive or pass the ball the length of the floor for the lay up. But if a defender flies or breaks a good distance toward his offensive goal, then 1 must play defense.

As in all of the passing-dribbling game, the important thing is to teach the players the whys, the whens, the hows, and let the players play within the framework of those do's and don't's.

THE PASSING-DRIBBLING GAME VERSUS
THE COMBINATION DEFENSES

Teams that resort to trumped-up defenses, such as the Combination Defenses, concede defeat before their game begins. Coaches who teach their teams these defenses tell their players they are inferior to their opposition and therefore are expected to lose. Negative approaches, such as these, almost never win.

There are three major Combination Defenses: the diamond and one, the box and chaser, and the triangle and two. By using the rules of the free-styling passing-dribbling game, none of these defenses present a problem.

The Diamond and One

Two guards and two baseline attackers fill the holes of the diamond. The man being chased is required to be a perpetual motion machine. The four men being zoned repeatedly break to and through the holes of the zone, and they constantly screen for the motion machine. Dribbling, except for the lay up or for penetration, should not be permitted. Quick ball movement while adhering to these do's and don't's will defeat the diamond and one.

The Box and Chaser

The passing-dribbling attack meets the box and chaser with a point formation. The two wings align behind the front line defense while a baseline attacker moves along the baseline or flash pivots into the middle of the box. The man being chased again becomes a perpetual motion machine. The point man should, expecially if he is tall, split the front line defenders, laying the ball off to the uncovered wing for either an easy jumper or another dribbling penetration. Each player must also screen for the man being chased.

The Triangle And Two

The Overload without the weakside exchange supplies an excellent answer to the triangle and two. The two players being chased play the 1 and 4 positions. This enables all of the options, especially the baseline screens by 3 for 1 and the inside rolls by 5 and 2, to get the high percentage shots.

First, by using the passing-dribbling game a coach teaches all his players to be offensively competent, making it difficult for any team to play a gang type defense against one or two attackers without hurting their overall defensive effort. Secondly, psychologically the game is ours because we know we can win and they know it too. Their coach told them so. Thirdly, we approach the defenses positively, thinking them no more difficult than any zone, in fact—weaker.

THE PASSING-DRIBBLING GAME VERSUS OUT OF BOUNDS DEFENSES

There are two primary out of bounds defenses: the zone and the man. It is difficult, if not impossible, to get the lay up against the zone. But it is easy to get the high percentage shot against the man. Because of this most teams have gone to zoning out of bounds play. Teams that still use the man-to-man drill on it sufficiently to eliminate the excellent shot. There are many variations of man-to-man and zone defenses. To be moderately successful against each of them would require teaching two or three out of bounds plays against each variety. Therefore we have deduced that working on out of bounds plays does not pay large enough dividends to justify the time spent to be successful. So we simply work to get the ball in-bounded prior to a five second violation. We also like for our movement to end in an Overload alignment.

Diagram 11-4 exhibits the above principles of attacking an out of bounds defense. Diagram 11-4 beleaguers both the zone and the man. It not only attempts to score but it will enable the offense to inbound the ball against all defenses.

4's break across the lane provides the initial option. Unless properly defended 4 has the lay up whether the defense is a man-to-man or some type of zone.

When facing a man-to-man defense, 5, the center, screens for 1, a guard. 3 checks X5 to determine whom he will pass to. If X5 switches, 3 hits 5 for the lay up. If X5 does not switch, 3 passes to 1 for the jump shot. 1 could switch responsibilities with 2 by screening for 2.

If the defense is a stay-home zone, 3 can lob a pass into 5 for the leaping jump shot. 4 helps by screening the middle man of the zone away from 5. Also to

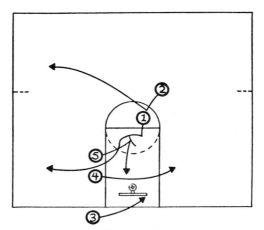

Diagram 11-4

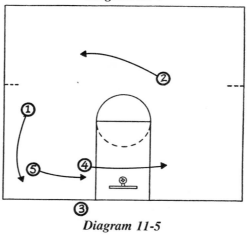

Diagram 11-5

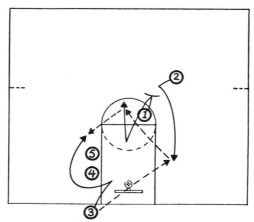

Diagram 11-6

get the ball inbounded against the zones, three attackers, 1, 2, and 5, will flood the right side of the court. 2 breaks to the midcourt area as a safety value. 1 breaks to the corner and up the sideline if he cannot get the ball in the corner. 5 breaks to the low post, and he continues out to the corner if 3 has trouble inbounding the ball.

If the ball is out of bounds on the left side of the basket, the players switch sides of the courts. They still have the same duties.

When 3 inbounds the ball, he breaks to the rebound area previously occupied by 4. 4 vacates to the point. 2 becomes the strongside wing man. 1 is at strongside corner while 5 mans the post. We now have the ball inbounds, and we are in the Overload formation, ready to attack whatever defense we are facing.

When we get the ball out of bounds under our basket with only a few seconds left in any quarter, we run our quickie out of bounds series. Both plays are designed to get the shot within a couple of seconds.

Regardless of the zone being faced we run the pattern displayed in *Diagram 11-5*. All zone defenders would have to cover 4, 5, and 1's slides in the manner described below.

4 still breaks under the basket, and if a defender releases him to another defender, it creates a temporary openning. So any mistake by the defense would give 4 the lay up. 5 breaks to the area vacated by 4. The defensive center had to cover 4. Now the defensive forward or cornerman must cover 5, the offensive center. Any exaggerated mismatch might be met with a lob pass. 1 fills the area 5 vacated. A pass to 1 gets 1 the jump shot. And no time elapses until the pass from 3 touches a player inbounds. So this pattern requires only a second.

If we have at least three seconds left and we have run our regular out of bounds play, we activate the pattern shown in *Diagram 11-6*. 1 screens for 2 and rolls. If 2 is open, 2 takes the shot. If 2 is not open, 1 pops back outside for a pass from 2. X3 would be expecting 3 to break across the lane as he did in Diagram 11-4. But 3 times his break around 5 and 4's double screen to correspond with 1's receiving the pass from 2. A pass from 1 to 3 gets 3 the jumper as 5, 4, 2, and possibly 1 hit the offensive boards.

THE PASSING-DRIBBLING JUMP BALL ATTACK

A numbering system, called by the jumper, informs all five players where the ball is going if we can control the tip. If we are unable to control the tip, or if we have doubts about controlling it, the same numbering system puts us in a clockwise or a counterclockwise rotation in an attempt to recover the lost tip.

The last digit of a two or three digit number tells where we will tip the ball. Three digits without a zero means we will undoubtably get the tip. And when we are certain beyond suspicion we want to fast break. Two digits means fighting for the tip without a fast break following. 24, for example, means we tip to the 4 o'clock area. 12 o'clock is directly ahead of and in the same direction that the tipper is facing. 243 would mean a tip in the 3 o'clock area with a three lane fast break following. So we start two men breaking as the referee releases his toss.

A three digit number with a zero in it means we will not get the tip. An even number calls for a clockwise rotation, and an odd number demands a counter-clockwise rotation. So 103 would mean we will not control the tip but we will try to gain possession by rotating counterclockwise. 404, for example, would be a clockwise rotation. The tipper should study where the ball will probably be tipped. Then he should call the proper rotation so that our players will reach the recovery spot as the ball arrives.

Whether we can control the openning tip or not, we want recovery of the ball, and we want the last possession of each quarter. It is most difficult to defeat a good team that has earned those four extra possessions each game.

THE GAME SAVING TWO-MINUTE DRILL

It has become a popular strategy for the offense to call time out with a few seconds left in a game and the score even or the offense a point or two behind. This strategy nearly always fails. When the offense takes the time out, the good defensive coach will not only anticipate what the offensive team will do, but he will inform his players, strengthening their chances of stopping the offensive play. Many times the defense will even change their team defense, momentarily confusing the offense thereby causing them even more problems.

It seems wiser not to take that time out, not to give the defense time to regroup. Our game saving two-minute drill has worked out in advance what we will do offensively in the last few seconds of the game. Also every attacker has the advantage of knowing what defense they have been facing the last several possessions. So the offense can attack a sure defense instead of an anticipated one. And the defense cannot call the time out without possessing the ball. Therein lies the importance of the two-minute drill.

To substansiate our belief in this strategy: we have never lost to a team that took time out in the dying moments of the game to either try to tie or to defeat us, but we have won many games by not taking the time out, by trusting our players to stay grouped as in the practiced two-minute drill, and by allowing our players to advance with the sure knowledge of the team defense facing them. In fact, when we were undefeated state champions, we won the regional championship game on a last second shot; and we won the state finals by not taking a time out after getting the ball with twenty-five seconds left and down by one point. We scored with thirteen seconds left, and our opposition took the popular time out. We knew whom they would go to in this situation, and we even anticipated the play. Without the help of that time out, we could not have relayed the information to our players. We also forced the inbounds pass to their weakest player and left their weakest shooter semi-open while tightly opposing their stronger attackers. Time outs work to the advantage of the defense, not the offense. Wisdom dictates teaching and making use of the two-minute drill.

We drill on a few quickies to be used against the opposition we play that week *(see Chapter 9)*, and the late game situation is a perfect spot for using one of those quickies. While practicing our two-minute drill, we inform our players which quickie we want used. Not only do they stay grouped, but the players attack with a certainty that comes from having drilled and re-drilled the play.

The Two-Minute Drill

Procedure

1. Five offensive players and five defenders.
2. We give one team (usually the defense) a point or two lead.
3. One assistant coach directs each team. Each squad is told which defense to employ if they are ahead and which defense when they are behind. The team with the lead stalls; the team behind fast breaks. The team with the lead runs the predetermined stall against the defense it faces; the team behind runs our passing game offense working for the good shot. Coaches or managers officiate the games, with each foul netting at least a one-and-one free shot. All the offensive properties of this text are put into operation by at least one of the squads. If a team is behind by a point late in the two minute period and regains control of the ball, they do not call time out, which would enable the other team to change defenses, but they attack with their pre-planned quickie.
4. We begin each two-minute session with a jump ball.
5. It can be made a one-minute drill if practice time is limited.
6. Coaches can repeat the drill, using the same or different strategy, as frequently as they wish. But the drill should be used often with each team practicing their quickies at least once.

Objectives

1. To teach team poise.
2. To teach alertness in tense situations to all players.
3. To teach players to stay abreast of the time remaining in the game.
4. To drill squad on what to do in the dying moments of a close game.
5. To teach strategy, creating a team with five playing coaches.
6. Because of the all out effort required, the two-minute drill is a game conditioner. Running the drill late in practice sessions corresponds with the tiredness factor of late game situations.

Our two favorite last second-quickies have scored on every occasion that we have used them. The time remaining when we reach midcourt determines which maneuver we use. Both quickies are used only when the score is tied.

If five seconds or less remain, the dribbling guard studder steps, trying to get his guard leaning in one direction. When the defender bends, the dribbling guard drives over the defender's opposite outstretched leg. He must be careful not to contact the defender in the torso. If possible, the attacking guard should get his head and shoulders by the defender before he stages the trip. Contact must result and acting must be sincere and appear real. Acting helps force the official to make the call. It would be best if the attacker could hit the defender with enough violence to propel both to the floor. Should this collision be judged a charge, the offense only loses possession of the ball with a second left, hardly time for the opposition to mount an offensive. But should it be called a block, and drilling will perfect the technique, the offense obtains the one-and-one and victory.

But if six to ten seconds remain and the score tied, the dribbling guard studder steps but drives completely to the baseline and leaps into the air, floating out of bounds. For some strange reason, defenders will not follow this guard across the baseline. At the exact moment that the dribbler cuts the corner, the post man rolls away from his defender into the lane, forcing his defender to play between him and the driver with the ball. The center lines himself up with his shoulder underneath and parallel to the basket, facing out of bounds. As the driver floats out of bounds, the post man screens his defender from the weakside, placing the post defender on the post attackers back. Because of the perfect defense being played originally by the defensive post man, a passing lane is open from the out of bounds guard to the positional post man. Once the post man receives the ball, he has a power lay up and he probably will be fouled. Should the defensive post player play between the baseline and the attacking post man, a pass back to a high cornerman and a reverse pivot by the post man gains the inside two footer. A team could not ask for a better chance to win.

A SECRET PASSING-DRIBBLING GAME SECRET

Let the players play on game night. The reader should do his coaching during practice sessions. Coach so that the players will be as well informed on strategy as they are on techniques. Never talk too much; players will work situations out for themselves. Coaches should only provide guidelines. The passing-dribbling attack not only accomplishes the above, but it is pure basketball, the type being played on the playgrounds of the world. Players learn best by doing.

Index

N